Enjoy the read, and always
embrace your truth!
                Best,
                Sharon

# THE TRUTH ABOUT THE LIES

WHAT WOMEN TELL THEMSELVES

THAT KEEP THEM STUCK

WITH CHEATING MEN

SHARON MATTHEWS FORTUNE

SMF media

© 2021 by Sharon Matthews Fortune

All rights reserved. No portion of this book may be reproduced, stored in a retrieval system, or transmitted in any form or by any means—electronic, mechanical, photocopy, recording, scanning, or other—except for brief quotations in critical reviews or articles, without the prior written permission of the publisher. Failure to comply with these terms may expose you to legal action and damages for copyright infringement.

**Library of Congress Cataloging-in-Publication Data**
Matthews Fortune, Sharon
    The truth about the lies: what women tell themselves that keep them stuck with cheating men/Sharon Matthews Fortune

Printed in the United States of America

First Printing, 2021

ISBN 978-1-7361737-0-1 (paperback)

Publisher's Disclaimer:
This book is not intended to be used as a substitute for psychotherapy or treatment from your personal mental health professional. Readers are advised to consult their own qualified health professional regarding treatment of mental health or medical conditions, as this book does not dispense professional advice. This book contains fictional characters. Characters and events are either the product of the author's imagination, perception, or interpretation. The information is not intended to diagnose, treat, cure, or prevent any mental health or emotional disturbance. In the event the reader uses any of the information in this book for personal circumstances, the author and the publisher assume no responsibility for your actions and outcomes.

# CONTENTS

Acknowledgements

Preface ............................................................................................. i

Overview: How We Cope ............................................................. 1

## PART 1 Lies "The Blind" Tells Herself ................................... 5
If Only I Had Proof ........................................................................ 7
All Men Are Cheaters .................................................................. 13
He Confessed So He's Ready To Change ................................... 17
She Means Nothing To Him ........................................................ 23

## PART 2 Lies "The Manipulator" Tells Herself ..................... 27
I'm Not Going To Give Her The Satisfaction Of Me Leaving Him ... 29
If I Stay He'll See How Much I Love Him And Stop Cheating ... 33
Because I Stayed After He Cheated Again He Owes Me ........... 37

## PART 3 Lies "The Finger-Pointer" Tells Herself ................. 43
He Cheats Because Of How He Was Raised ............................... 45
He Cheats Because He's Influenced By His Friends .................. 49
He Cheated Because She Came After Him ................................. 55
He Cheated Because I ___ (Fill In The Blank) ........................... 59

## PART 4 Lies "The Dreamer" Tells Herself ............................ 63
He'll Change After We Get Married ........................................... 65
He'll Change After We Have A Child ......................................... 69
He'll Change After We Go To Counseling ................................. 73
He'll Change After He Recommits To The Church .................... 81

## PART 5 Lies "The Helpless" Tells Herself ............................. 85
He's All I Got / I Don't Want To Lose Him ................................ 87
I Feel Stuck .................................................................................. 91
I Don't Want To Start Over ......................................................... 97
He Knows How Much He Hurt Me So He Won't Cheat Again ... 103
Maybe This Is God's Will For My Life ..................................... 107

## PART 6 Lies "The Settler" Tells Herself .............................. 111
At Least I Know What I Have With Him ................................. 113
Being With My Cheating Man Is Better Than Being Alone ..... 117
I Don't Care Anymore So His Cheating Can't Hurt Me ........... 121

| | |
|---|---|
| PART 7 Lies "The Savior" Tells Herself | 125 |
|    I Want To Save My Relationship | 127 |
|    I'm A Christian So I Have To Forgive Him | 131 |
|    I Don't Want To Break Up My Family | 135 |
|    I Have To Give Him A Chance To Change | 141 |
| PART 8 Lies "The Compromiser" Tells Herself | 145 |
|    He Takes Care Of Me | 147 |
|    Everybody Has To Deal With Something In Their Relationship | 151 |
|    As Long As He's Respectful With His Cheating I Don't Care | 157 |
| Epilogue | 161 |

# ACKNOWLEDGEMENTS

My gratitude to my friend, Edward Broaddus. First, he was willing to share his multitude of talents to assist with making my dream of becoming a self-published author a reality. Furthermore, he freely gave his time encouraging and motivating me to stay accountable to my goals. I thank him for all the technical expertise that shepherded this book through the publishing process. I cannot put into words how grateful I am that he committed to this journey with me from day one.

My gratitude to Lisa Y. Burrus is more than I can express. She jumped in with both feet, sharing her invaluable insight, and didn't stop until this book was perfectly polished. Her time commitment to both developmental and line editing was immeasurable. Lisa's ability to understand the author's meaning and express it clearer, keen eye for details and flow, and creative approach to structure, added tremendously to the allure of each chapter. I thank her for taking on this project and for all her hard work and dedication.

Similarly, there is no "thank you" big enough to acknowledge the contribution of my amazing daughter Cameron, and friend Samond. They passionately challenged my ideas for the book cover with an unwavering commitment. I immensely enjoyed the many hours spent listening to their feedback, which assisted with clarifying my vision and creating an intriguing finished product. I also thank Cameron for the many other ways she supported me in getting this project completed. I love you dearly.

# PREFACE

Women have stayed in relationships with cheating men unaware of the lies they tell themselves that cause them to feel pain. I wrote this book specifically for you if you are feeling defeated thinking you can fix things, yourself included, so your man will stop cheating. This is not a guidebook on how to leave your cheating man and not intended to belittle you for staying. By the end of The Truth About The Lies, you will be able to identify and change the thoughts and behaviors that have kept you stuck.

This book is for you if:

- you have abandoned your value system to stay with a cheating man,

- you have lost yourself in a relationship with a cheating man,

- you have attempted to control or taken responsibility for your cheating man's behaviors,

- you have buried the truth so deep in your soul that you no longer know what it is.

This book is especially for you if your man has repeatedly cheated.

Working as an agent of change in my psychotherapy private practice, I began noticing a common pattern of thinking shared by women who were in relationships with cheaters. Intelligent, articulate, intuitive women of all ages and races were struggling and telling themselves the same lies that for me had been all too familiar. As I listened to them and attempted to assist with the process of change, I repeatedly heard the common lies they were telling themselves. The more they resisted the truth, the more compelled I felt to write this book.

Embracing the truth is difficult. It is not an automatic shift, and it does not happen overnight. It is a process. We have a tendency to become storytellers when we don't want to face our truth. There is a storyteller in all of us. As storytellers, we arrange events and facts according to our thoughts, and use those stories to understand and to make sense of our world. Stories lead us outside of ourselves into a maze of details, guiding us further away from the truth we are trying to avoid.

Let's start with my truth. I have been cheated on. I know what it is like to stay in a relationship with a habitual cheater. I have distorted the truth, denied the truth, and avoided the truth. I lied to myself. Lying was necessary because remaining in a relationship with a habitual cheater did not fit into my moral code, my value system, or my self-image. The lies I told myself about why I was staying kept me stuck with cheating men.

I have only been in two long-term relationships with habitual cheaters, and both were men with admirable qualities. Everyone, including me, believed they adored me and I was in an ideal relationship. However, I would eventually come to realize that being adored did not guarantee monogamy. Instead of accepting reality, I began circumventing the truth. In my version of the story, these admirable men would eventually stop cheating, and I would then have the ideal relationship. In hindsight, I realized the truth was unacceptable, and by circumventing the facts, I could choose what I wanted to deal with until they changed. At least that was what I thought. The truth is, until you deal with the lie, the truth will deal with you. The truth deals with you through your emotions (sadness, anger, and fear), your behaviors (fighting, arguing, and manipulating), and your thoughts (worrying, plotting, and suspecting). What I know is the truth is always active, even when you attempt to tell yourself a lie.

Telling the truth about the lies I had created led to an epiphany. All the hurts and betrayals I blamed the cheating men for making me feel were self-inflicted. I was guilty of hurting and betraying myself by staying with the cheaters. This revelation was so powerful it led me to accept the truth. Did the

## Preface

cheating men stop cheating? No. Did I live differently? Yes. The result was one of obtaining a level of peace I had never experienced.

Accepting the truth led to everything being reversed one hundred and eighty degrees. All the changes I had been waiting for the cheating men to make were changes I needed to make. How could I expect them to respect my boundaries if I kept moving the boundary lines with each violation? I had to respect my boundaries, respect my values, and respect the truth to respect myself. In the end, the truth was all that mattered.

*The Truth About The Lies* is not based on an individual woman's experiences. I base it on shared perceptions common to women who have lied to themselves and stayed stuck with cheating men. It is not to be mistaken for therapy or the results of a research study. Read this book to assist with realizing the lies you have told yourself about your reasons for staying. Through reading this book, I hope you will arrive at your place of truth. Your peace is awaiting you in The Truth.

# OVERVIEW: HOW WE COPE

There are things that all women have in common, but no two women are exactly alike. As unique as we all are, there is a cluster of common patterns of thoughts and beliefs that contribute to staying stuck in relationships with cheating men. Listening to a girlfriend, family member, or client sounded all too familiar. The woman on the talk show, the co-worker needing an ear, and the conversation I would overhear while standing in the grocery line all fit into little boxes. I became curious and desired a deeper understanding about the patterns, the boxes, and us as women.

I kept asking myself what it was about being cheated on that made us develop similar coping mechanisms that in reality were doing something to the contrary? Instead of coping, we were lying to ourselves and holding onto distorted realities while resisting change. Of course, this was occurring without acknowledgment. As I worked through my stuff and worked with others towards self-awareness, I labeled characters for the common patterns of thoughts and beliefs that fit nicely into eight ways of coping. I wrote this book about the characters because it is easier for us to see things when we step outside of ourselves. It enhances the possibility of being able to see our beliefs and actions in the characters and to identify the coping mechanisms that have worked against us in the past.

The lies we tell ourselves are like editing a script for a movie to make it reflect what we want to see. The writer can do this with a movie script because it is fiction. When we attempt to do this with our lives, it results in us becoming a character and playing a role in our relationship drama. This is not how life should be lived. We should live our lives in reality and not through fiction. When we allow things we would rather not accept in our lives, we cope as a character image of ourselves to avoid the truth. Allow me to introduce my concept of the characters that manifest as we continue to lie to ourselves.

## "The Blind"

I think it is most befitting to start with "The Blind." This title fits because no matter how many times she stumbles over things and runs into walls, "The Blind" is incapable of seeing what is right in front of her. Eventually, she learns to maneuver around things by using her senses. She senses that something is there but just cannot see it. Acting blind when it is obvious her man is cheating is a coping mechanism that leads to lies that keep her stuck without acknowledging that she is choosing to stay with a cheater.

## "The Manipulator"

As "The Blind" gains clear sight of her situation, she gives birth to "The Manipulator." To manipulate, according to Webster's Dictionary, means *to use or change something in a skillful way for a particular purpose.* As she develops into "The Manipulator," she becomes very skillful at using and changing information, facts, and beliefs. This helps her to cope with the situation and to stay with her cheating man. Unlike "The Blind," she sees exactly what is going on and fully acknowledges that her man has cheated. When she copes by becoming "The Manipulator," she uses his cheating to get what she wants. She attempts to create a win for herself when she has lost the one thing that she wanted most, to be with a man who holds her in high regard and never cheats.

Do not be mistaken, "The Manipulator" is no pushover. Her primary goal is getting what she wants by any means necessary. She is crafty and calculating with her acceptance of his cheating. Although she is accepting what she does not want or approve of, she accepts it only as a means to an end. She thinks she is smart and knows exactly what she is doing. What she fails to realize is she manipulates herself more than anyone involved. That keeps her stuck.

## "The Finger-Pointer"

"The Finger-Pointer" has perfected the art of placing blame. She too acknowledges the fact that her man has cheated. The problem with this way of coping is it never leads to holding the cheater responsible for his actions. Instead, she

## Overview: How We Cope

seeks others to blame rather than trying to deal with the real problem, her man. She is every cheating man's dream because she will always exonerate him from his guilt. With her, the cheating man is the victim of an inescapable situation, and it relieves him of any personal responsibility for his actions. Keeping the finger pointed in the wrong direction keeps her stuck.

### "The Dreamer"

"The Dreamer" knows her man is cheating. However, unlike "The Manipulator," she is not interested in using his cheating to her advantage. She is also not like "The Finger-Pointer" who blames everyone and everything else for her man cheating. "The Dreamer" sees "potential." Yes, the wonderful illusion of potential that traps some of the best of us is what she uses as a coping mechanism. She lives partially in fantasy while dealing with her reality. Yes, her man is cheating, but she believes that he has the potential to change after some "future experience" takes place. We base dreams on what we desire in our lives, and she will take a chance. She believes he will stop cheating "when _____." You fill in the blank, almost anything will fit, and that is the lie that keeps her stuck.

### "The Helpless"

To be helpless means being unable to control something, protect oneself, or make a situation better. That is exactly how "The Helpless" copes with her man's cheating. She feels a lack of control over the circumstances happening in her life, and she cannot change things to her satisfaction. There is plenty that she could do, but she focuses on what she does not want and cannot imagine doing. What "The Helpless" fails to realize is the fact that she is the author of her fate and not her cheating man. Her self-imposed helplessness intensifies her immobility, and this keeps her stuck.

### "The Settler"

"The Settler" is a bit different from "The Helpless." While "The Helpless" views things from the point of view of what she does not have and does not want, "The Settler" copes by sorting through the mess to see what of value remains. "The Settler" looks for security in accepting less than what she wants, needs, or desires. She chooses not to risk walking away to create exactly what she deserves. Instead, she finds comfort in adjusting to the cheating by accepting the positively negative life that they can have together.

## "The Savior"

What exactly does a savior do? "The Savior" comes to the rescue. She comes to rescue the relationship from failure. She seeks to redeem the cheater from his destructive ways and guide him and the relationship to its ideal state. "The Savior" takes responsibility for fixing what is broken, restoring what is damaged, and reviving what has died. She believes it destines her to "serve" and not to "deserve" which keeps her stuck sacrificing her happiness forever.

## "The Compromiser"

Finally, "The Compromiser" is quite interesting. She is a little blind, a bit of a dreamer, and a settler all rolled up into a practical way of thinking that results in her becoming "The Compromiser." She is blind because she chooses carefully what she wants to see. "The Dreamer" in her sees the potential for a minimal amount of harm instead of the reality of ongoing betrayal. Her ability to settle creates comfort in positive aspects of negative situations. What makes her "The Compromiser" is she accepts that if she gives up something she wants, she will end up with some of what she needs. She has a way of blending the ideals of the relationship she wants with the flaws of the relationship she has. This creates the perfect coping mechanism for the cheating, but it keeps her stuck.

As you read, you may recognize yourself as possessing one, two, or a combination of all eight of the character coping styles. Learn from your own experience. Read with yourself in mind, and focus on your stuff to reveal the lies that you may still tell yourself. Laugh, cry and shake your head, but commit to telling the truth.

# PART 1

## LIES

# "THE BLIND"

## TELLS HERSELF

# IF ONLY I HAD PROOF

The more things change, the more they stay the same. Cheating has existed as far back as history goes, and the signs have changed little over time. Even though technology has elevated the cheater's game to a new level, the basic signs remain the same. Still, despite all the obvious evidence, "The Blind" will need proof that her man is cheating. She will stay with her man because she has never "officially" caught him cheating.

Her girlfriend's man works late all the time and does not answer his phone when she calls. "The Blind" tells her there is no doubt he is cheating. Her cousin's man disappears for hours, sometimes days, and re-emerges with a crazy alibi. She raises her eyebrows, knowing for sure that her cousin's man is cheating. Her coworker tells her she found a condom in her man's drawer, but he said it belongs to a friend. She shakes her head at how gullible her coworker must be to believe this obvious lie. Why can't "The Blind" see her own man's cheating as clearly as everyone else's? When similar things are going on in her world, why is it not proof her man is cheating?

"The Blind" will say she needs proof that her man is cheating, but when she is tripping over the evidence and the red flags are waving like windshield wipers, she cannot see the obvious. Let me share with you why this happens. "The Blind" becomes a master at minimizing and rationalizing her cheating man's behaviors because she does not want to accept the reality. His alibis are as weak as water and transparent as glass, but she analyzes the facts until lost in a haze of irrelevant, self-imposed questions that steer her away from dealing with the truth.

The lie, "If Only I Had Proof," is dangerous because being blind makes her doubt her better judgment. She thinks that maybe she is over-reacting mainly because her cheating partner plants seeds of doubt. Asking logical questions that demand straightforward answers and challenge inconsistencies, results in him calling her insecure, paranoid, or crazy. To believe the lie she tells herself about needing proof of his cheating, she has to make some changes to protect her sanity. This is how her blindness comes into being.

"The Blind" may become super busy and pre-occupied with activities, events, and work to assist with creating the blind spots that lead to ignoring, denying, or analyzing away the proof of her man's cheating. She may become vague and defensive when her girlfriends question her man's alibis. Even though she might resort to seeking proof that her man is cheating, she usually collects the evidence without connecting the dots. She convinces herself, and anyone questioning, that her lack of action is justified because until all the pieces of the puzzle are in place there is no proof that her man is cheating. Therefore, she blindly goes on with her life because she does not want to deal with the truth.

As long as she is blind, her cheating man is virtually safe to continue being the cheater he is. The Truth is, she never really wanted proof of his cheating. What "The Blind" wants is to be in a relationship with a faithful man. Having proof of his cheating is a threat to her future. As long as she does not have proof, she gets to stay in the relationship and not feel like a fool or stupid and used. This could go on forever, and the longer it does she becomes more empty and bitter. It roots her emptiness and bitterness in her knowing the truth, but maintaining the lie.

Now let me clarify something. You may read this and denying that you are "The Blind" because you challenge your cheating man when his alibis are weak. When he shows up late, cannot be located, or acts suspicious, you have no problem challenging him with a list of questions. You have no problem letting him know what you will and will not accept, and you will threaten to leave him in a heartbeat. I never said that "The Blind" was a pushover or a doormat. I simply pointed out the fact that she is coping by becoming blind to the obvious signs of his cheating. She sets clear boundaries, but because she is blind, she continues to trip over the boundary lines, stumbling away wounded.

This is not the first time that her man has cheated, and she stayed. Her blindness progresses because he is a repeat offender. Progressive blindness helps her deny she might have made a mistake when she stayed. In reality, it disappoints her that she stayed because this does not fit into her self-image. Her blindness will not allow her to see things as they are because staying with her cheating man violates her value system. Instead of working on changing herself into a woman who lives in truth, she seeks to change the way she sees the relationship. She needs to believe that she did not make the mistake of staying with him against her better judgment.

For a moment, let's shift the focus to what proof "The Blind" has. She has proof that the relationship is not fulfilling and does not make her proud to be with her man. It does not meet her needs, she is sad more often than happy, and she cannot trust him to be faithful. She has proved he is not committed to telling her the truth and is not committed to their relationship. He has shown her who he is, and she has ignored the obvious because it does not agree with the lies she has told herself for so long.

I started this chapter by stating that the basic signs of cheating have changed little over time. Even "The Blind" can sense when something is wrong, out of place, or out of sync. When blind, if something in the environment changes, you sense the difference. Below are some signs and behaviors common to cheating men. Use the list to sharpen your senses and help lead you to accept the proof that your man may be cheating.

## **Signs and Behaviors Common to Cheaters**

<u>Changes in Work Habits</u>

- Working longer/later hours
- Working weekends when he normally doesn't
- Inconsistent changes in his work schedule

<u>Need for Privacy</u>

- More secretive
- Putting passwords on phone/computer

- Leaving the room to talk on the phone
- Hiding cell phone or keeping it on silent
- Concealing phone records

## Changes in Social Life

- Spending more time with a new friend
- Attending more activities without inviting you
- Not interested in doing anything with you
- Spending more time on the phone, computer, texting

## Changes in Accountability

- Can't be reached when out/not answering the phone
- Staying out late/coming home late
- Staying out all night
- Not where he said he would be
- Not with whom he said he would be with
- Telling you he's coming over and not showing up

## Changes in Mood

- Bored with you
- Short-tempered towards you
- More negative towards you

- More defensive when questioned

## Changes in Intimacy

- Considerable reduction in the frequency of sex
- No passion when having sex
- Not interested in sex at all
- Problems getting/maintaining an erection
- Introducing new positions

## Changes in Finances

- Less money despite working overtime
- Money missing or unaccounted for
- Unexplained credit card charges/purchases

## More Attention Given to Looks

- Change in style of dress/frequently purchasing new clothes
- Changes in grooming habits
- Joining a gym/increased interest in body image
- Coming home from work smelling like soap/cologne

Now let's be clear, these are only signs of cheating, not proof. However, if you have stayed with your cheating man having seen these behaviors in the past, these are more than signs. This is proof that "The Blind" has chosen not to see. If she bases leaving on having proof of her man's cheating, she would need to look no further. The Truth is, she never intended to acknowledge the proof because then she would have to do what she fears. She lies to herself because she fears leaving one cheating man and ending up with another cheater. Worse, she fears being alone. The Truth is, as long as she acts as "The Blind," she will not be alone. She will stay stuck with her cheating man until she accepts the proof that lay right before her eyes.

# ALL MEN ARE CHEATERS

How many times have you heard it said that all men cheat? If we polled every woman in the world, I believe a large majority would agree. In the minority, rightfully, you would find "The Blind." She enters a relationship feeling that she has thoroughly assessed her new man's morals and values. Care is put into choosing him following a courtship comprising deep conversations. This provided her with information needed to peer into his personality, character, and habits. They have thoroughly discussed her stance on cheating, and he knows beyond the shadow of a doubt cheating would be a deal-breaker. Yes, she made it clear if he cheated, the relationship would be over. Since they addressed this topic, she feels certain that cheating will not be a problem she and her man will have to conquer.

Even though her man confessed to cheating in his past, he assures "The Blind" that he would never cheat on her. He may have taken his loyalty a step further and nobly professed that if he ever much as thought about cheating, he would leave instead. This left her with no worries, and she firmly believed they had this issue under control. That is, until she catches him cheating. Let us take a moment and recap events. "The Blind" meets a man, and through a series of conversations learns about his history of cheating. She informs him that cheating is a deal-breaker, he professes his loyalty, she believes him, and then he cheats.

She is in shock because her man, who admitted to a history of cheating, has now cheated on her. She simply cannot believe he would do this to her after he professed he would not. How could this happen after all the deep conversations and the peering into his character, personality, and habits? Did she miss something, misjudged his character, or misunderstand his intentions? Her confusion gives way to a haze of irrelevant questions and analyzes that render her blind to the fact that her man is still the cheater he told her he was in the past.

# The Truth About The Lies

Blinded by the haze of confusion that she creates amid obvious facts, she does what most warm-blooded woman would. She turns to "her girls" to assist with solving this puzzle. When they all see the obvious, that she is not ready to see, she moves on to other advisors; perhaps her pastor, a relationship counselor, or the self-help community. Because she is "The Blind," there is no logical way for her to comprehend the fact that a cheater who she carefully chose has now cheated on her. Any advice that points out the obvious is swiftly disregarded, and she presses forward, seeking to find the missing pieces to the puzzle that her disbelief has created.

Once mentally drained, she will inevitably entertain the women in the majority who believe that all men are cheaters. These women share their experiences with their cheating men that led to their blindness. The answer to her puzzle, according to the women in the majority, is simple. They convince her that her man cheated because all men are cheaters. She need not look any further; her puzzle is solved by "the majority."

Now let us be clear, there are two types of men. There is "The Man Who Has Cheated," and then there is "The Man Who is a Cheater." These two men are very different in action and character. "The Man Who Has Cheated" may have had a lapse in judgment and fallen prey to a situation he did not know how to escape. "The Man Who Has Cheated" might have been in a state of mind that impaired his judgment and ability to think rationally. He might have blurred his boundary lines and crossed over into uncharted territory. "The Man Who Has Cheated" might even have underestimated his willpower to remain faithful by any means necessary. He made a mistake, and now he realizes that all men are humanly susceptible to cheating under the right circumstances.

Looking at his character, "The Man Who Has Cheated" has etched into his value system the belief that cheating is wrong. He is truly sorry for his actions. Amid shame for his transgressions, he seeks forgiveness. He is humble, remorseful, and willing to do whatever it takes to rebuild the trust in the relationship. This man takes full responsibility for his actions and struggles to forgive himself for his wrongdoing.

In "The Man Who is a Cheater," you will find very different character traits. For him, cheating has become a default behavior, a recurrent pattern, and a force of habit. He has not fallen prey to a situation, nor had a lapse in judgment

## All Men Are Cheaters

that lead to his cheating. This man is the one who seeks a situation conducive to cheating. "The Man Who is a Cheater" has loose boundaries and maneuvers in and out of them easily. He does not struggle with things like willpower when it comes to cheating; he does not intend to be faithful for long and has cheated on multiple partners.

"The Man Who is a Cheater" can always justify his acts of cheating, and under the right circumstances, he believes cheating is acceptable. Cheating is not a violation of his value system, and his conscience is dull to the destructive nature of being unfaithful. He is a bit egotistical about cheating and believes it justifies him to cheat if women do not satisfy his needs. When caught, he can always tell his woman exactly what he was missing that led him to cheat, which normally places the blame on her. It is extremely difficult for him to identify a means of getting his needs met aside from lying down with another woman.

"The Man Who is a Cheater" may act humble, but not for long. He will more than likely become defensive when caught cheating rather than accept responsibility for his actions. This man is subject to lie several times before admitting even the smallest measure of the truth. He will not spend much time re-hashing the facts, so his woman will have to get over his cheating quickly and move on. "The Man Who is a Cheater" is more interested in his woman addressing what she has done wrong in the relationship than him identifying ways to regain her trust. He is not interested in soul-searching questions that will help him understand the core reasons he continues to cheat, and therefore he will remain a cheater.

The Truth is, all men are susceptible to cheating, but all men are not cheaters. When "The Blind" buys into the lie that all men are cheaters this makes her susceptible to inappropriate behavior, and that weakens her boundaries. Once she violates her boundaries, it complicates her ability to justify the belief in her values. Before the blindness set in, she told her man that cheating was a deal-breaker. Now that she has embraced the lie that all men are cheaters, it makes no sense to leave. Cheating gets re-evaluated and measured by the degree of discretion and involvement versus her old value system that rendered it absolutely, unacceptable. Accepting the lie that all men are cheaters devalues her worth. The belief that she deserves to share an exclusive, monogamous relationship with a man who doesn't cheat because it is a part of his value system diminishes.

"The Blind" needs to remove her blinders and see her man for who he is. Boys cheat because of raging hormones, emotional immaturity, and a lack of clear values. Men who are cheaters are no different. They are simply showing signs of emotional immaturity and a faulty value system. The men who turn into cheaters do so because there are women who permit them to cheat. In the beginning, she said that she would not tolerate cheating, it was unacceptable, and she would leave if he cheated. Instead, she stayed with him, opting to dishonor her boundaries and values, which led to her being stuck.

The Truth is, "The Blind" is guilty of two things. One, she entered a relationship with a man with a history of cheating and believed him cheating on her to be impossible. When he cheated, she acted as if she could not believe this was happening. Why, because she thought there was something special about her that would magically cleanse him of his cheating spirit. The second thing she is guilty of is she never asked him if he shared her beliefs and values about cheating. Entering a relationship with a man who has a history of cheating no doubt increased her chances of being cheated on. Some say the past is the best predictor of future behavior. If a man defaults to cheating every time something goes wrong in the relationship, his needs are unmet, or he feels the urge, please take the blinders off and know that he is a cheater. Her man, not all men, is a cheater. Believing the lie that all men are cheaters keeps her stuck.

# HE CONFESSED SO
# HE'S READY TO CHANGE

Just because you are blind, it does not mean your senses are not on point. "The Blind" has been experiencing a nagging feeling that something is not right. Repeatedly, she asked her man what is going on behind her back, if there is anything he needs to tell her, or if there is someone else? She struggles to see but remains in the dark. Tracking inconsistencies in his answers when questioned is the norm and increases her level of suspicion. The fact that he will not answer his phone when she calls, will not answer his phone when it rings in her presence, and will not give straight answers when questioned makes her believe he is cheating. Despite her suspicions, he maintains his innocence.

"The Blind" just cannot seem to shake the sinking feeling something is not quite right. Even though she continues to tell herself that there is no proof of her man cheating, she knows he is not being completely honest. She is not paranoid, insecure, or crazy, but she is suspicious. There is an old saying, "everything done in the dark will soon come to the light." She is a firm believer that sooner than later the truth will come to the light.

Without being questioned, quizzed, or probed, one day her man comes to her with a confession. He wants to talk, and she has never seen him look so serious, bothered, or guilty. Her heart races because she knows that whatever he has to say will not be good. What she has been searching for all this time has found its way to her. Her man is finally ready to be honest, to tell the truth, and to confess to his wrong. Yes, "The Blind" is about to receive a surprise, and after all her investigating and interrogating, she never expected him to come clean.

Not only does her man confess to cheating, he is also more than willing to answer all of her questions. Maintaining her cool, she rolls out the questions quickly and concisely. She is careful not to interrupt the flow of information by tripping about what she is hearing. His patience with her is almost admirable as he allows her to review all the mental notes that confirm all her past suspicions. He provides all the missing pieces to the puzzle for all of his disappearing acts, late nights out, and sudden changes in his work schedule. "The Blind" has all the proof she needs that her man has been cheating.

If this were his first time cheating, it would not be fair to label her "The Blind" for believing his confession meant he was ready to change. Since he has cheated before, the label suits her well. In her defense, the first time she confronted him with suspicions of cheating, things played out differently. The first time signs of his cheating surfaced, he was defensive, irritable, and manipulative. He denied everything she thought she knew and called her paranoid, insecure, and crazy. Despite her persistent probing, he did not confess, and she probably acted paranoid, insecure, and crazy. He reluctantly confessed to something insignificant, such as flirting, but bullied her into believing there was no proof of him cheating. She stayed with him, but not without suspicion.

The first time she caught him cheating his apology for the limited dirt he vaguely admitted was weak. Even with hard evidence, he maintained his innocence. He answered questions, but in a vague, guarded manner, refusing to admit to anything that would seal his guilt. He consistently told her that certain facts were irrelevant and shut her down by becoming frustrated and angry. When his guilt was finally sealed, he was more interested in "putting it behind" and "moving forward" than answering a battery of questions. To quote him, "talking about it over and over ain't doing nothing but keeping us stuck," and then he stopped answering questions.

When caught cheating the first time, his words and actions were not consistent. He said he wanted a chance to fix things, make it up to her, and be a better man. All that followed was telling her she needed to stop asking questions, work on the things that made him cheat, and accept he was a changed man. She stayed because she wanted to believe his words and believed that everyone makes mistakes. Hoping to learn to trust him again, she stayed and prayed he would be true to the change he promised.

Now you can see why "The Blind" believes that this current confession means he will stop cheating and is ready to change. This confession differs greatly from the past where he defensively denied everything only to admit to being minimally involved with someone else. We can see how she would buy into the lie that her man is ready to change because he is showing a side of himself she has never experienced. Although angry and disappointed, wanting to slap him and hug him simultaneously, she finds it within herself to give him credit for being honest and owning up to his wrong. She pulls out her blinders, disregards all of her histories with him, and believes he has had an enlightening experience rendering him ready to be the honest, faithful man she always wanted.

For "The Blind," this current confession creates a battle between her head and heart. While her heart tells her to give him yet another chance to change, her head tells her not to believe the hype. Careful not to forgive and move on too soon, she reaches out to "her circle" for advice. The suggestions range from, "take a chance on love," to "don't be a fool again," to "stay but keep your eyes open." After many days of being distracted, and divided by the decision at hand, she settles on the belief that he confessed so he is ready to change.

Here is how she has earned the label "The Blind." By definition, confessions admit to something taking place and confirm involvement. A confession is a release of information once withheld, denied, or concealed. Additionally, a confession is choosing to reveal information that will seal your guilt. What a confession is not is evidence of a person's readiness to stop a behavior or their ability to change their character. Sometimes a confession might be a first step in contemplating a change, but one would be blind to believe that a confession means her man is ready to stop cheating.

Because a confession is usually the first step towards contemplating a change, staying sets "The Blind" up for a long, winding road that hopefully will end in change. Unfortunately, change is not automatic. He is going to need a grace period to think, feel, and act as a faithful man. Because she stayed, and we always protect our decisions, she will have to become "The Blind" to deal with his slip-ups, lapses in judgment, and straight-up poor decisions. After all, he is still the same man with a history of cheating. Just because he confessed to one transgression does not mean he is now a changed man.

To strengthen her decision to give him another chance because of the belief that his confession means readiness for change, "The Blind" creates a story. The story starts with her fantasy that he has finally grown up and has come to his senses. She adds that he confessed because he respects her enough to protect her from hearing about his cheating in "the streets." It continues with her embellishing a higher level of respect for him because of his honesty. She concludes the story, deciding to believe that he is ready to change. By telling herself there comes a point and time in every cheater's life when he tires of playing games, this story assures her that her man is ready to stop cheating.

The Truth is, "The Blind" does not know why her man confessed to cheating. She believes his confession means he is ready to stop cheating and become a changed man. If the confession was for the right reason, then he may be ready to change and stop cheating. Then, and only then, will the confession lead to the next step in the process of change. After contemplation, there comes preparation. He would prepare to change by doing some introspection and reflecting on what he needs to do and/or stop doing to be faithful. He would go further and prepare to be honest in all his dealings as to hold himself accountable for his actions.

I believe the most important step in the process of change is self-examination. Without her man doing some soul-searching to get an understanding of why he cheats, how to discipline himself from opting for immediate gratification, and working to revamp his value system, he will probably cheat again. She should not lie to herself and rush in to believe that his confession means the end of his cheating and readiness for change. Change, like the decision to cheat, comes from within. The decision to be faithful comes from a commitment to change, and consistency measures commitment. If he puts in the work, his potential to stop cheating increases.

What should the preparation for change look like? He may do obvious things like change his cell phone number, shut down social media, and give her full access to all his gadgets. Taking it a step further, he would challenge behavioral, social, and communication patterns that set him up to cheat. She would probably see him change the places where he hangs, the people he hangs with, and the frequency of hanging out. Her man would likely include her in plans, outings, and events. She might even notice that he is easier to talk to and less secretive. These things should give "The Blind" a sense of hope that her man is on the path to change. If there is no change, and she still believes he is ready to stop cheating, then she is lying to herself.

Everything listed above reflects external changes, and we know that genuine change happens within. These external changes are a good start, but they are only changes in habits and patterns. The Truth is, a change of heart and a change of beliefs is the only way that her man will change the character traits that have led him to continue cheating. If "The Blind" wants to assess her man's readiness to change, she needs to watch what he does and listen to the words he speaks. If she is vigilant, her man's actions and words will eventually reveal his true intentions. The Truth is, she will remain stuck with her cheating man if she does not look for more than a confession as evidence of his readiness to change.

# SHE MEANS NOTHING TO HIM

When "The Blind" thinks about the woman that her man cheated with, she likes to think of her as his mistake. She considers her a slut or whore, a woman with loose morals, who was only there for a good time. Therefore, she is meaningless to her man. "The Blind" cannot see this woman as having any actual value to her man because of her belief that "she means nothing to him."

The other woman cannot mean anything to her man. After all, she knows him inside and out, or at least that is what she thinks. She has analyzed, evaluated, and interpreted his behaviors for so long she feels like a pro at reading him. "The Blind" can detect when he is mad, disappointed, hurt, or happy. She can predict what he will do in certain situations and how he will respond to certain comments. Even though from time to time he has thrown her a curveball, and has done something that catches her off guard, she knows her man loves her.

Remember, even though she is blind, her senses are still quite keen. She has picked up some risky behaviors on her radar. She knows that he has a wandering eye, can be flirtatious, or just too darn friendly. He is overly accommodating and attentive towards other women. "The Blind" warned that he would end up in something that he would not know how to get out of if he did not change his ways. She told him that his flirty and accommodating nature would lead to something he would later regret, and it did. He cheated, just as she sensed he would.

With eyes wide shut, she evaluates, analyzes, and interprets his actions. "She means nothing to him" is what "The Blind" concludes. After all, she had already predicted that his flirty and accommodating ways would get him into trouble and lead to regret, so this woman means nothing to her man. He ended up having sex with her because he did not know how to get out of the mess he had created while flirting. To stay with him, "The Blind" has to make the other woman a non-factor.

Because she has made the other woman a non-factor, all she has to do is help her man to see how he made his mistake.

She pounds in his head the need to stop flirting, to stop being so darn nice, stupid, and accommodating. All he needs to do is learn to think before he acts. That is the remedy to his cheating. "The Blind" convinces herself that because her man loves her, the other woman cannot possibly mean anything to him. She is firm in her belief that it was just sex.

To deepen her convictions, she commences to raking the other woman over the coals and dragging her through the mud. "How could she mean anything to him, look at her, she's not his type, she looks like a slut, stripper, trash!" "She's too old-fashioned or too ghetto for him, and she doesn't have a degree, a good job, or has nothing to offer, so she can't mean anything to him." The chatter in her head tears down the other woman so she can sustain her belief that this woman means nothing to her man.

It is time to take the blinders off and time that she faces the truth. She needs to admit that the other woman is meeting some need her man has chosen to not fulfill with her. The other woman exists because he wants to be with her, not because she means nothing to him. Just because "The Blind" believes the other woman means nothing to him, does not make it the truth. The other woman means something to her man, and that is why he continues to cheat.

Can "The Blind" withstand a bit more of the truth? She should ask herself whether her man genuinely loves her and determine whether his actions feel like love. Is it the time invested in the relationship that makes her believe she is the one who means something to her cheating man? She should ask herself what she means to him before she goes on believing the other woman means nothing. "The Blind" believes because she and her man are still together, it means he loves her. Has she ever considered what the other woman thinks "The Blind" means to him? Whose man is he anyway?

"The Blind" does not realize that two things have taken place. She has bought into a love triangle, and she is a part of a three-strand cord between herself, her cheating man, and the other woman. In the love triangle, her man is at the top, and "The Blind" and the other woman are at the bottom in opposite corners. As long as she believes the other woman means nothing to him, it is all right for her to stay with her cheating man. She will continue to reduce the other woman to "nothing" so she can stay with him with a shred of dignity.

A three-strand cord is strong and not easily broken. This type of cord will last a long time and endure pressure. This is her story with her cheating man and the other woman. Her blindness will not allow her to see the bond he has with the other woman and how he has wrapped himself around them both. "The Blind" does not even realize that her refusal to face the fact that the other woman means something to her cheating man is allowing him to maintain his bond with them both. The three-strand cord and love triangle will endure the pressure of confrontation and allegations because she continues to believe the lie that the other woman means nothing to him.

I do not know how many times I have sat with a beautiful, intelligent woman, in a counseling session, who adamantly believes that the other woman means nothing to her man. Despite the mountain of evidence to the contrary, these women will not face the truth. Their men have lied about discontinuing communication with the other woman, and they know that to be true because they have checked phone logs, text messages, and social media. Their men have lied about not spending time with the other woman, and they know this because they have stalked him with tracking devices on his vehicle and phone, or stumbled upon incriminating evidence. Evidence reveals he has maintained regular communication with the other woman, and he continues to spend time with her. "The Blind" ignores the truth that the other woman must mean something to her man.

I have to flip the script here to remove the blinders. It would surprise "The Blind" to hear what a counseling session with the other woman reveals. The other woman calls her stupid, desperate, and weak for staying with a man who she knows is cheating. She says you mean nothing to him; he is not sleeping with you, feels sorry for you, and does not love you. He tells her the two of you are roommates, and he is only there for the children or financial reasons, and she believes the lie. Whatever the reason, the other woman believes you mean nothing to your man because he loves her. How can two women be suffering from the same blindness? Could it be because neither of them will tell the truth? They continue to lie about the other's worth, and they stay stuck because he means something to them both.

"The Blind" sees the other woman as her man's mistake, while the other woman sees "The Blind" as her man's misery.

## The Truth About The Lies

Neither of them can see "The Truth" which is they have both created lies about one another to make themselves feel loved by a cheating man. Neither of them can see the three-strand cord because they do not believe there is anything that binds him to the other. The cheater is in a relationship with them both, but neither can comprehend his actual attachment to the other because of self-imposed blindness. Both "The Blind" and the other woman stayed with him, believing he would soon tire of "her," or "she" would tire of his mess and leave. As stated earlier, this type of three-strand cord will endure pressure, and the love triangle could continue for a very long time.

The Truth is, if "The Blind's" cheating man loves her, he does not honor her. His connection to her is faulty and allows for continuous disconnection. He might love her enough to not want to leave her, but not enough to care about the impact that his cheating has on her well-being. If he loves her, he does not love her enough to be honest, and not enough to let her go if he cannot be the man that she needs. The Truth is, she needs to see her man simply does not love her enough.

When she is ready to see The Truth, it will reflect the obvious, which is her cheating man loves himself far more than he loves her and the other woman. They both mean something to him, but he means more to himself. As we look at the triangle that the three have created, "The Blind" and the other woman are at opposite corners at the bottom. They elevate their cheating man to the top and in the center of both of their lives. They have to reach up to him, and he has to come down to them. Taking off the blinders will allow them both to see that he does not think too highly of either of them, and the one getting all the love is the cheating man.

The biggest measure of The Truth for her to accept is he does not love her enough, and neither does she love herself enough. Loving herself would allow her to tell the truth. The Truth is, she does not love herself enough to walk away from a man who maintains a relationship with a woman who "means nothing to him." She does not love herself enough to unbind from the three-strand cord that will endure as long as she is blind. Ultimately, she does not love herself enough to elevate from the bottom corner of his life where she shares space with the other woman. "The Blind" should work on loving herself instead of trying to prove that the other woman means nothing to him. Until then, she will stay stuck with her cheating man.

# PART 2

# LIES
# "THE MANIPULATOR"
## TELLS HERSELF

# I'M NOT GOING TO GIVE HER THE SATISFACTION OF ME LEAVING HIM

This scenario is all too common. Your man is cheating, and the other woman decides it is time you know. Somehow, she finds your phone number and calls. You cannot believe her boldness; who does she think she is? She calls expecting that by putting you on notice, you will leave "her" man alone. Now of course this news scrambles your thoughts, but as soon as you regain alertness, your wheels start to turn. She expects you to leave him because she told you about them, but you decide that you will not give her the satisfaction!

Normally, by the time the other woman contacts you, her relationship with your man has already run its course. Her goal is to make you leave him because he will not leave you. Either she has noticed him growing bored with her and pulling away, or she tires of waiting for him to leave you. Whatever the case may be, he has not left you, and she wants to destroy what you think you have.

Shock and anger give birth to "The Manipulator." She skillfully takes the information from the confrontation with the other woman and changes lanes strategically making "her" the issue. How did "The Manipulator" allow the actual issue, which is her man's cheating, to dodge the bullet? How did the other woman become the target instead? Well, it makes perfect sense when you are "The Manipulator," and the intent is to use the other woman to get what you want from your cheating man. The other woman's punishment for opening her mouth will be to watch you stay with your man despite his cheating. "The Manipulator" intends to show the other woman exactly how irrelevant she is. "She" deserves a thank-you card for granting you this opportunity to scheme your way into control.

"The Manipulator" has risen, and she is ready to spin the facts to fit her own needs. Is she concerned about her man's cheating? Yes, but she is more interested in proving a point to the other woman. Her cheating man created this situation, the

## The Truth About The Lies

other woman revealed it, and "The Manipulator's" goal is to win. The plan is to reclaim her territory by making him leave the instigating other woman, so that "The Manipulator" will be the one to get the satisfaction.

The Truth is, "The Manipulator" does not realize she is manipulating herself more than anyone else. Her man gets the luxury of her efforts to entice him away from the other woman, and the other woman gets the attention that she was looking for when she made her presence known. All "The Manipulator" gets is the inconvenience of wearing herself out by plotting and scheming. The other woman has now taken up residence in her head and is draining all of her positive energy. He reaps the benefits of her competing for his affection, and she gets to keep a cheating man. Where is the satisfaction in this scenario?

She masterminds ways to show the other woman that her cheating man has recommitted to her. The other woman's intent was, and continues to be, to move "The Manipulator" out of the picture and claim her place. Now "The Manipulator's" intent not to give the other woman the satisfaction of leaving has created a false bond with her cheating man. What exactly has "The Manipulator" accomplished by "not giving her the satisfaction?" She gets absolutely nothing more than she had before; she is stuck with her cheating man.

What would she be giving the other woman if she left him? Is "The Manipulator" really in any position to give the other woman anything? After all, it was her cheating man who gave himself to the other woman in the first place. It is up to him to give himself back to her and give her the satisfaction of him ending the affair. This is the only satisfaction she can manipulate out of this messy situation. It is too bad she does not understand this and will spend far too much time and energy manipulating herself.

The Truth is, by leaving her cheating man she would not be giving the other woman any satisfaction. What she would give her is a cheating man. She would gain her satisfaction from knowing that now the cheating man is the other woman's headache. There is no way the other woman will have any peace with him, so "The Manipulator" would be giving her the multitude of worries. Let the other woman spend her days and nights wondering where he is, whom he is with, and what they are doing. Let her hold the title of "his woman" and then wear herself out trying to be enough to prevent him

# I'm Not Going To Give Her The Satisfaction Of Me Leaving Him

from cheating. What she would give the other woman is the satisfaction of becoming "The Manipulator." History will repeat itself, he will cheat on her, and some "other woman" will call to make her presence known. Now that is true satisfaction!

Unfortunately, her preoccupation with scheming keeps her from seeing what satisfaction would come from letting the other woman have her cheating man. After all, she is not staying because she is in love with him, nor is she staying because she wants to work on improving their relationship. She is staying mainly to prove a point to the other woman, and she uses her cheating man to that end. What "The Manipulator" gets for her efforts is continuous dissatisfaction with her own love life.

The Truth is, coping by becoming "The Manipulator" will cause her to be insecure, vengeful, resentful, and bitter. She may win her cheating man away from the other woman, but all she wins is an unhealthy relationship. Love is not what is motivating her to stay, nor is it a belief that he will change. The thing that keeps her with him is the lie that she tells herself about staying to avoid giving the other woman satisfaction. If she would be truthful with herself and admit that she will not receive any satisfaction from competing for a cheating man, she could create satisfaction from disconnecting from this drama.

On the flip side of the manipulation is the fact that she intends to make her cheating man stay with her. She should ask herself a few questions. When was the last time that he was all hers? Can she make him stay with her? When he cheated in the past, what satisfaction did she get from staying? Does she believe he will stop cheating if he leaves *"this"* other woman? "The Manipulator" should only want him to stay with her if he is truly ready to commit, and she is ready to forgive. That is her only hope of getting any satisfaction.

As stated before, there is a saying that goes, "the best predictor of future behavior is past behavior." This man has cheated before, and manipulating him into staying now will not change his cheating character. Instead of creating drama by attempting to "not give her the satisfaction," why not focus on what she desires from this situation? A man who has cheated, but has now committed to change while recommitting to her, is what "The Manipulator" really wants. Staying with a cheating man to prevent the other woman from getting satisfaction is a pointless use of her time.

The other woman's purpose in her life is singular - to bring to light the fact that her man is cheating again. The other woman is simply a reflection of his character flaws. She is only a symptom of a preexisting problem between "The Manipulator" and her cheating man. He has cheated before, is cheating now, and probably will continue to cheat because this game does not address the actual problem.

The Truth is, "The Manipulator" will continue to play games that do not require a genuine change from her cheating man. She will never gain satisfaction from staying, and he will never change as long as women compete for his affection. This game will always feed the cheating spirit in her man, and she will stay stuck fighting for what should be hers in a healthy relationship. The only way for her to stop manipulating herself is to give up the lie; she is not withholding satisfaction from the other woman by staying with him. The Truth is, the only one "The Manipulator" is withholding satisfaction from is herself by choosing to stay stuck with her cheating man.

# IF I STAY HE'LL SEE HOW MUCH I LOVE HIM AND STOP CHEATING

This lie is a common manipulating factor behind why many women stay with cheating men. The cycle goes something like this, he cheats; she finds out; he says he's sorry and never meant to hurt her; she is distraught and initially unforgiving; he says "she" meant nothing to him. Next, the cheater begs, pleads, and stalks. He professes his undying love for her, says he cannot imagine life without her, and he falls apart every time she tells him it is over. He refuses to let her go and will not stop persisting. She mistakes all of this for love and readiness to commit, which leads to her staying. This is where the lie starts. Ultimately, she believes her loving act of staying will stop his cheating. Yes, she aims to manipulate the cheating right out of her man.

"The Manipulator" is sadly mistaken if she believes that her demonstration of love will stop his cheating. The fact that he begged, pleaded, and stalked means that he already knew that she loved him before, during, and after he cheated. She cannot comprehend the fact that once again it is all about her cheating man and his wants. It is all about what he desires and thinks he deserves. He manipulated his way into another chance with her, and she intends to return the favor by aiming to manipulate the cheating out of him.

Morphing into "The Manipulator" because of emotional wounds has caused her to lie to herself and believe something that is not likely to happen. Why does she now believe that she can control her cheating man's actions by staying with him? Hasn't she already done that; wasn't that what was going on when he cheated? Wasn't she loving him before and during his cheating? Why would choosing to stay with him after he has cheated again now somehow be a magic cure? What she does not realize is she is manipulating herself more than him, and this keeps her stuck.

## The Truth About The Lies

She is setting herself up for the ultimate failure by believing the lie that her love will cure her man of his cheating. What will happen is "The Manipulator" will now have to work even harder to keep his affections. After all, isn't that how she will show him how much she loves him? She will have to do things, say things, and give things that will show him how much she loves him to keep him from cheating. What a lucky man he is. He cheats and now reaps the benefits of extra attention and affection from her as she aims to show him how much she loves him to stop his cheating. Who's manipulating whom?

"The Manipulator" is calculating and crafty. She plots a strategy to make herself look like the perfect martyr. Everyone will see her commitment to making the relationship better and will tell her cheating man how lucky he is to have her. His friends will tell him he needs to "get his act together" and be the man that she deserves because "The Manipulator" will strategically do, say, and be all that any man has ever desired when in their company. Yes, she has strategically developed a choir that will sing her praises every time her man so much as thinks about looking at another woman.

Now, this is not the first time "The Manipulator" has suspected or confirmed her man's cheating. I say this to show that she has already tested the theory of her love having the power to control his urges to cheat. She should ask herself if her love for him can grow deeper and deeper, with each discovery of his cheating, before it works as a catalyst for monogamy? The Truth is, her man is staying with her because he already knows how much she loves him. However, this will not cause him to stop cheating.

Coping with her man's cheating by becoming "The Manipulator" is costing her because obviously, her love for him has never been enough. If her love were the thing he needed and wanted, then he would not have cheated. Becoming "The Manipulator" requires her to step her game up 100%. She has become preoccupied with how she looks, what she wears, and what she does. She has to plan extravagant dates, prepare extraordinary meals, and have excessive sex. The choice to manipulate has worked in the reverse. Because she stays and manipulates her man into seeing how much she loves him, hoping he would stop cheating, he gets to reap rewards from his inappropriate behavior.

The old saying goes, "don't start anything you don't plan to continue." When will she have done enough to prove to him how much she loves him so he will stop cheating? There is no end to the manipulation. Now that she has ventured into the role of being his "every woman," there is no turning back. She has provided him with a one-way ticket to paradise. Any change from her extravagant, extraordinary, and excessive way of doing things will give him the liberty to cheat again. She is stuck in a cycle of manipulation because of scheming instead of breaking away from this never-ending, no-win situation.

The Truth is, this act is not who she really is. There is no way to love someone when you are not your true self. Love grows from security, authenticity, and congruency. Love will not result from scheming and manipulating. She knows in her heart that she can never give genuine love to someone she cannot trust. What will grow from scheming and manipulating is vulnerability, fear, and neediness. Attempting to manipulate him into not cheating again will leave her emotionally drained.

It is not unusual to hear about women going into debt, or spending money they do not have, to pay for expensive gifts and trips to show their cheating men how much they love them. The cheating man loves every minute of the attention because, after all, it has always been about him getting what he wants, what he needs, and what he desires. Unfortunately, none of this guarantees he will stop cheating. "The Manipulator" ends up broke and broken-hearted when her man cheats again. The Truth is, staying has shown that all of her gifts and gestures have no power over his choice to cheat. All of her failed efforts should have proven that no woman has the power to stop a cheater from cheating. Only he can control that.

All the efforts she has channeled into trying to change him with external motivators have failed because change comes from within. External factors will not result in lasting change and do not have the power to change a person's internal makeup. Because of this, she feels used, unappreciated, and devalued. She cannot believe he could cheat again, considering all she sacrificed and manipulated to make him see how much she loved him. This leaves her enraged and stuck in an abyss of bitterness. As said before, coping through becoming "The Manipulator" is a setup for failure.

The Truth is, becoming "The Manipulator" has no real or lasting benefits. What she wants is a man who will love her enough not to cheat. She wants a man who will not cheat because of who he is, not because of who she will become to keep him. "The Manipulator" wants a man who appreciates her love for him, and in return, loves her back. She knows that she does not have this in him, but is not willing to tell herself the truth. The Truth is, genuine love and manipulation cannot exist at the same time. Staying without telling herself the truth keeps her stuck with the lie that her love can stop his cheating.

## BECAUSE I STAYED AFTER HE CHEATED AGAIN HE OWES ME

Previously, "The Manipulator" vowed to show her man how much she loved him, believing her decision to stay would have the power to stop his cheating. When she realized staying had no control over his cheating, the script was flipped. The new lie she tells herself is about what he owes her, because she stayed. She feels that because she stayed, it entitles her to his faithfulness. This lie gives her a sense of power over her situation that in reality does not exist. Redemption is her goal, and she intends for her cheating man to pay dearly.

In all of her craftiness, she thinks that staying after her man cheated again has created a debt for him to pay. She lies to herself and creates the belief that her cheating man will now do whatever it takes to keep her. "The Manipulator" is so busy scheming and plotting that she misses the obvious facts. If he wasn't putting her on a pedestal and doing what it takes to keep her, after he cheated the first time, what makes her think that he will commit to doing anything differently now? If she wasn't his number one priority after he cheated the first time, what makes her think she will now hold that position? Her thinking is not logical because she is allowing her emotions to rule.

What is more likely to happen because she stayed after he cheated again? He is likely to join in on the manipulation. He sees some value in keeping her or else he would have let her leave. If he does whatever it takes to keep her, love and commitment won't be the motivating factors. Her cheating man will do what it takes to keep her for his selfish gain and benefits. Choosing to stay with him won't result in her having the man she wants; one who values his relationship with her so much that he will never put himself in a position to lose her. What she will gain from staying is a cheater who will plot and scheme right along with her so he can continue to get whatever he needs from her.

## The Truth About The Lies

Let's revisit the definition of manipulation shared in the Overview, "to use or change, in a skillful way, for a particular purpose." Her purpose in staying is not to heal her wounds through working to develop a deeper level of love, nor is it to restore her trust in him. Her purpose is to get what she has always wanted, and that is for him to value her enough to do whatever it takes to make her feel secure in their relationship. She wants a man who will do whatever it takes to keep her because of his love for her, and she intends to get that man by any means necessary. The Truth is, her man will never be that man, and she refuses to accept that fact.

In the beginning, when she first discovered he was cheating, she was outraged, disgusted, and angered. She didn't want to hear anything that he had to say. She couldn't stand the sight of him and didn't care about his rationale for cheating. All she wanted was for him to crawl back into the sewer he came from and leave her alone. In the beginning, anger blocked all of her manipulative juices, and she just wished that she had never wasted her time with this jerk. She wanted to move on with her life and to forget that he ever existed. Then a spark of negative energy fueled by retribution and redemption ignited in her, and she vowed to get back everything that he had cheated her out of in their relationship.

"The Manipulator" lies to herself by thinking that her man's cheating has provided her with the golden opportunity to get exactly what she wants. She sees the opportunity in this crisis to erase all the embarrassment and pain that his continuous cheating caused. Now she will allow him to prove to everyone who pitied her how much she means to him by allowing him to cater to her every need. She believes that she can finally get exactly what she always wanted from her relationship because she stayed after he cheated again, and he owes her.

In reality, her true intention is to get him to honor her lists of wants, needs, and desires. The same list that she has preached, pleaded, and bargained for throughout their entire relationship is what she expects him to buy into now because she stayed after he cheated again. Until now, he has virtually danced, skated, and maneuvered around her wants, needs, and desires while pleasing only himself. He called her needy and said that her expectations were unrealistic, assuring her that no man would jump through hoops to be in a relationship with her.

Now she lies to herself and believes that his cheating has provided her with an opportunity to make him eat his words.

The Truth is, what she seeks is control, and she believes she is now in the position to give demands, create orders, and command attention. Normally, the cheater will cooperate for a brief time because he sees some benefit in keeping her around. Because he has something to gain from being with her, he will initially honor her demands, orders, and commands. He will be her puppet and allow her to pull and yank his strings for a moment. This makes her feel she has gained control of his actions and will have everything she has always wanted.

All good things eventually come to an end, as will her manipulative powers over his actions. For the cheater, this act has an expiration date. Did "The Manipulator" fool herself into thinking that she could control her cheating man forever? Did she not know that he would grow tired of having his strings pulled and catering to her demands? Did she think that his cheating and her staying created an entirely new script? Did she lie to herself about the quality of the relationship she now has potential to have? Anything manipulated will eventually revert to its authentic form.

While in the fog of her schemes, "The Manipulator" forgot that there was a time, not too long ago, when her man thought she was too needy and expected too much. He hasn't changed and has been trying to manipulate her while she was trying to manipulate him. He has been trying to manipulate her into staying with him because he has attached value to keeping her around. She couldn't see this because she was too busy trying to manufacture a relationship with a cheater where her needs would mean as much to him as his own. She never envisioned that he would "play" her because she desperately needed to believe she could get what she wanted because she stayed after he cheated again.

Reality sets in as she helplessly watches her man revert to his true character. Her attempts to manipulate him into a man with genuine intentions to attend to her needs, wants, and desires have failed. His interest in manipulating her into thinking he could be transformed into the man she wanted has ceased. Now the relationship is right back where it started as he shows her he doesn't feel he owes her anything. He's back, the one who told her she was needy and her expectations were unrealistic.

## The Truth About The Lies

Now she has no choice but to open her eyes and see the problem that has always existed. "The Manipulator" has to face the truth that she has no control over her man's actions. The Truth is, she wanted to make all that her man had put her through worth her time and investment. The lie she told herself about him owing her because she stayed was her way of creating a reason to stay. Her attempt to manipulate him into being someone whom she knew he could never be was simply an investment in her partner of choice. She desperately needed to turn things around so she would not have to face The Truth about the time and energy lost staying with him.

If she could tell herself The Truth, she could then admit that the manipulation was a waste of time. She would have to admit that her attempt to control him had proven that he was not willing to change; he did not feel he owed her anything for staying. She would have to accept the fact that because she dug her heels in deeper, she became the needy, clingy woman that her man said she was. If she could finally face The Truth, she could see that he was right about her expectations of him being unrealistic. The Truth is, he proved that he would not make any authentic changes to be in a relationship with her.

"The Manipulator" needs to get to The Truth by asking herself some hard questions. Could she forgive his cheating if he acts as if he owes her? She should ponder whether she could securely stay with him if he shows he feels he owes her? Could the debt be repaid? Finally, "The Manipulator" should clarify the question of what her cheating man owes her for, the cheating or her staying? The Truth is, he cheated, and that is what he had control over. She stayed, and that is all she had control over.

The Truth is, she gave her control to him when she decided his future actions would make her choice to stay with him worth her time. She gave up control as soon as she went against her moral compass and attempted to manipulate him into being what she wanted in a partner. The push-pull began when her moral compass and his were not pointing in the same direction. No matter how much he will do, give up, or put up with the fact that he cheated would always be a moral dilemma for her and not him. It is obvious cheating is permissible according to the values that guide his decisions.

Speaking of demands, orders, and commands, she laid out the blueprint he was to follow. He wasn't able to stop cheating because of who he is at the core. As a result, she created a guidebook to help him reset his compass. The guidebook looks a bit like this:

- You promise never to cheat on me again.

- You will answer your phone every time I call.

- You will be home no later than _____.

- You will call me if your plans change.

- You will let me know if "she" calls you again.

- You will let me check your cell phone, text messages, and social media.

- You will give me access to all of your passwords.

- You will keep your phone visible, unlocked, and on.

- You will change your phone number.

- You will let me know where you are, who you are with, and what you are doing at all times.

    The desperation of "The Manipulator" is clear. It's also clear that she knows her man cannot be faithful without a guidebook. She knows that if she doesn't provide him with a concrete list to use as a guide, he will continue to do what he has always done. For her, this list reflects the commitment she wanted from him after he cheated the first time. However, for him, this list simply reinforces his belief that her expectations are unrealistic. He will reject this unrealistic list of demands because he said that nobody was going to jump through hoops to be in a relationship with her.

    The Truth is, if she took the time to heal from the hurt and disappointment, there would be no need for manipulation. Also, if she would take the time to reflect on what she truly wants in a partner and the relationship, she will see that he is not willing, nor able to deliver. She would realize that his cheating has nothing to do with him needing guidance, but has everything to do with his morals and values. Further, she would realize that she cannot control his morals and values, therefore she has wasted her time trying to manipulate him through her list of demands. "The Manipulator" will know The Truth when she realizes that by staying she has been manipulating herself the entire time. Until then, she will stay stuck with her cheating man.

# PART 3

## LIES

# "THE FINGER-POINTER"

## TELLS HERSELF

# HE CHEATS BECAUSE OF HOW HE WAS RAISED

We've all heard the clichés, *"the apple didn't fall too far from the tree, like father like son, and monkey see, monkey do."* There is no shortage of opinions and research about the influence of family dynamics on character development and behaviors. Various theories, from the beginning of time, have hypothesized a direct link between what we observe and how we behave. It is easy to make a good argument for the belief that behaviors are affected by the way family conditions us. However, at some point, the power of choice has to be a factor in the argument.

Repeated exposure to behavior has the potential to influence one's actions. I will not dispute the fact that observation can lead to imitation, after all that is one way of teaching children. I will even support the theory that we pass behaviors down from generation to generation. However, I will not support the lie, "he cheats because of how he was raised." "The Finger Pointer's" man is not a child who doesn't understand right from wrong. He can control the choices he now makes as an adult.

"The Finger-Pointer" is protective of her cheating man. She chose him and has to make sense of her decision to stay with him after he cheated. She is a master at rationalizing his behaviors and minimizing his role in the messy decisions that he makes. The biggest problem is this lowers his accountability for his choices and actions. She presents a case that renders her man incapable of making conscious choices about his cheating because of how he was raised. She sees him as a helpless victim of a generational curse that has plagued the men in his family from the beginning of time. In her opinion, if all the men in his family are cheaters, it only makes sense that he cheats.

"The Finger-Pointer" is happy to take on the role of

being her man's moral role model to restructure his value system. She plans to teach him how to value her and their relationship. Therefore, she believes that she will erase all the mess from his past that led him down the dreadful path of becoming a cheater. "The Finger-Pointer" also plans to expose her man to a multitude of honorable, respectful men who she considers admirable because they do not cheat. Her radar will be on high alert to shield him from all that might influence him to cheat. What she aims to do is raise a grown man all over again. I wish her good luck with that!

If she believes her man cheats because of how he was raised, and she knows he has cheated on every woman he has dated, then she should know there is nothing that she can do to reset his moral compass. He is who he is. He is not a cheater solely because of who raised him. He cheats because to him it is acceptable behavior. He cheats because he chooses to cheat, he can cheat, and she will accept his cheating.

Since we are placing blame, let's look at her role in his cheating. By lying to herself about why he cheats, she is cosigning his justification. Surely, before they became serious about their relationship, they discussed how she felt about cheating. There was also a discussion about his relationship history. If he was honest with her about his history of cheating, and she continued to date him, she in principle cosigned her future with her cheating man.

In all of their discussions, he probably never said he thought cheating was unacceptable. Because he was honest about his cheating history, she mistook this honesty as growth and assumed he'd changed. She thought the disclosure meant he was prepared to be in a mature, mutually exclusive, monogamous relationship. She formed her own beliefs and decided for herself what it meant for their relationship. "The Finger-Pointer" never asked her man if what she thought lined up with his intentions.

Just how does "The Finger-Pointer" normally find out about her man's family background as it pertains to cheating? It's a process. She notices signs of cheating and confronts him. She clarifies that cheating is a deal-breaker, and she will leave if she finds out he's cheating. He hears her, but he is who he is, so he continues to cheat until caught. Once caught, he pours out his heart and soul and claims he is helpless to the generational curse that has been cast upon him by the long line

## He Cheats Because Of How He Was Raised

of cheaters in his family. He claims he had no positive role models and swears his upbringing brainwashed him. If she had known all of this beforehand, she would have never gotten serious with this man.

"The Finger-Pointer" is in a serious relationship with a womanizer who is honoring his family's tradition of habitual cheating. Her man pitifully confesses that he does not want to act this way, but he cannot help himself. She buys into the lie he cheats because of how he was raised, and she believes she can help him change. If it were not for those wild dogs that raised him, he would have a chance at being a decent partner. His immoral relatives are responsible for his cheating ways, and now she is going to reform him from the negative habits that he inherited.

She stays because she understands how easy it is for her man to cheat because of how he was raised. She lies to herself believing she can reprogram his "learning" and teach him her morals and values. Everyone can change, and "The Finger-Pointer" believes that if she can just keep her man away from poor role models, he too can change. Just like the repeated exposure to the cheaters in his family tainted his values, she believes that the repeated exposure to her way of thinking and behaving can reverse the curse. He cheats because of how he was raised; he will stop cheating because she is going to raise a grown man all over again. She believes that her love and the re-programming will lead to him changing.

There is no respect for the cheaters who raised him. She secretly despises them, they disgust her, and she would rather he have no contact with them. She thinks they are immature, selfish sinners and should be struck down by God for their transgressions. These men are the scum on her tile, the dirt on her shoe, the burn on her toast, all of which are useless and undesirable. She feels all of this towards the men who raised her cheating man but sees him as an innocent victim. If he is acting like the men who raised him, then isn't he the same immature, selfish, useless, and undesirable sinner that should be struck down by God for his transgressions?

The Truth is, genuine change comes from within, and any change that results from external motivation will not last. "The Finger-Pointer" is wasting her time. She will have to change her man's value system because cheating is not wrong in his world. She will have to accept more cheating while she attempts to reform him because she knows that change doesn't happen overnight. She will have to abandon her value system and dismiss cheating as an unacceptable deal-breaker while attempting to change him. The Truth is, she will be stuck in his world while trying to make him an acceptable part of hers all because she refuses to hold him accountable for his choice to cheat. None of this will feel good to her, but because her focus is on why he cheats instead of the fact that he cheats, she will stay stuck in the discomfort.

# HE CHEATS BECAUSE HE'S INFLUENCED BY HIS FRIENDS

"Finger-Pointers" have adamantly blamed their man's friends for his choice to cheat. She thinks if only she can keep her man away from them, and if only they would stop influencing him, then he would stop cheating. The problem with this rationale is she believes her man is not responsible for his own choices and behavior. She sees her man as a victim of circumstances rather than a cheater, therefore she will not hold him accountable for his actions. Even though this is not how "The Finger-Pointer" had envisioned her life with her man, she will stay to help him change into the man she wants him to become.

So, how had she envisioned her relationship with him? There was probably magnetic chemistry when they first met, the kind that made her feel like a teenager. They probably spent hours talking on the phone, and he probably sent the most thoughtful text messages throughout the day. He was probably fun, romantic, and charismatic. She considered him "a keeper" and couldn't wait to introduce him to her circle. Everybody loved him and thought they were a cute couple, a perfect match for one another. All of her girlfriends envied her for finding such a handsome, intelligent, attentive man; she fell for him fast.

This was the start of a perfect relationship, or at least that was what she thought. Her man was eager to introduce her to his crew. She had heard all about them and knows that when he's not with her, he's with them. They are "his boys," and they accept her into the fold with open arms. They tell her man what a catch she is, and he'd better treat her right. As "his boys" get more comfortable having her around, she notices some red flags amongst the group. One has a wandering eye, the other is a big flirt, and his closest friend is a straight-up player. "The Finger-Pointer" is initially cautious with her opinions as she shares her observations with her man. She can't shake that nagging feeling that they are a bad influence on her *innocent* man, and she doesn't want their ways to rub off on him.

Eventually, she will meet the women who date his friends. This will be an opportunity for her to gather more information about them and to see how they treat women. The one with the wandering eye requires constant reeling in by his woman. The flirt and his woman argue repeatedly about his inappropriate and disrespectful ways. The player simply shows up with a different woman every time with each of them thinking that she is the only one. "The Finger-Pointer" is mortified that these are the men with whom her man spends most of his time. She is sure that they will eventually corrupt him and ruin her good relationship.

Her fears have come home to roost. She cannot believe it when she finds out that her man has been lying for his boys. The frequent calls to get him to provide a false alibi are simply irritating, and she wishes they would stop making him a part of their mess. She wastes no time letting him know how she feels about his involvement in their cheating, but he assures her that there is no need to worry. She never stops to notice the issues that should have caught her attention, which is the ease that her man rolls a lie off his tongue and the fact that lying does not bother his conscience. Because her finger is pointing in the wrong direction, she never recognizes the true character of her man shining through.

The more she knows about his boys, the less she likes. They are all cheaters, and she feels it's time for her man to stop playing boyish games with them and their women. When challenged about how easy it is for him to tell lies, and how it doesn't even appear to register as wrong, her man assures her he's just being loyal to his friends. She warns him that if he keeps hanging with them, their ways will eventually rub off and create major problems in their relationship. She gets more and more irritated when he is with his boys and attempts to block him from connecting with them so often. By filling her man's schedule with events that do not include his boys, she believes she can stop their colluding and reduce the negative influences.

Anyone with half a brain knows her attempts at keeping her man from his boys will never work. No matter how long he works, how tired he professes to be, or how late it is, her man

## He Cheats Because He's Influenced By His Friends

will always find the time to hang with his boys. She is not a dumb woman; she knows there is more than one way to skin a cat. So, she decides if you can't beat them, join them. The old saying, "keep your friends close and your enemies closer" is her new motto.

An all-out infiltration attack begins. She invites them to all of her events, plans for frequent group dates, and centers celebrations around her man and his boys. She lies to herself and believes that as long as she can keep an eye on her man, then she can save him from the "cheater" path that his boys have him headed down. This will be a never-ending battle because his boys don't want to hang around with her any more than she wants to hang around them. His boys will always maneuver out of her plans and take her man with them. "The Finger-Pointer" still has her gaze fixed on the wrong target. As long as she is plotting and scheming to save her man, she will never see the truth. He is a part of the problem and not a victim of his boys' habits.

Dancing around questions sheds light on the problem. Once she grows tired of the games, lies, and alibis, she confronts her man point-blank. The big questions finally roll off her lips. She asks if it bothers him that his friends cheat and if he thinks cheating is wrong. Beginning the dance, her man simply states that what his friends do is none of his or her business. Seeing him swirl around the question, she swirls with him and again asks if he thinks cheating is wrong? Her man dips out by saying that they are grown men who can do what they please. The ultimate question spins out, and she flat-out asks her man if he is cheating? He ends the dance by telling her he is done talking. She now sees a different image of him emerge, and his innocence tarnishes.

It never once dawned on "The Finger-Pointer" until now that her man might already have fallen prey to the influence of his messy boys. As they say, "birds of a feather flock together." She grows suspicious about what he is doing while his boys are approaching women. There is no doubt in her mind that women have approached him, and his friends have attempted to hook them up. She is connecting the dots, but she is still not drawing a straight line. While she is getting the picture that her man might be guilty of something, she still isn't seeing him as the initiator of the wrong.

"What's done in the dark comes to light." "The Finger-

## The Truth About The Lies

Pointer's" suspicions have led her to dig a bit deeper, uprooting a trail of lies that lead to the discovery that her man is cheating. Instead of dealing with the problem head-on, she takes the approach of a parent chastising a child who should have known better. She preaches about warning him that his friends would rub off on him. Then, she reminds him of how many times she has warned that his friends would get him into trouble if he kept lying for them. Still not able to see his true character, she is totally frustrated because she believes he has finally allowed his friends to influence him to cheat.

Let's be clear, someone can end up in a messy situation that they can't escape, and end up doing the wrong thing. It is also possible to be in the wrong place, at the wrong time, with the wrong person, and end up doing the wrong thing. Acting on an impulse and regretting it later is a part of human nature. However, this is not what her man is guilty of doing. She is using all the above to defend her choice to stay with him by denying that he is the captain of his ship.

She'll believe that he cheated because he didn't want to look weak around his boy or be criticized or teased. She will also hold fast to the belief that he cheated because he gave in to the pressure. The Truth is, "The Finger-Pointer" should look at the flip side of all of her beliefs. Her man didn't want to look weak to his boys, but didn't mind looking dishonest and unfaithful to his woman. He didn't want to be criticized or teased by his boys, but didn't mind disappointing and betraying his woman. She believes they pressured him into cheating, but she should look at the fact that she was pressuring him to do the opposite. Why didn't that stop him from cheating? The Truth is, at the end of the day her man made a deliberate choice to cheat because of who he is, not because of being influenced by friends.

More focusing on the truth would lead her to admit that she doesn't want to see the actual picture. It's easier to believe that she has a good man who is influenced by bad men who cheat. She doesn't want to accept the truth; her man made a conscious choice to cheat because he is a cheater. Is he a nice guy? Yes. Does she have fun with him? Yes. Is he getting enough sex from her? Yes. Is she his woman? Yes. Does he choose to be with her? Yes. Does he have another woman? Yes. Is he nice to her? Yes. Do they have fun together? Yes. Does he get enough sex from her? Yes. Is she his other woman? Yes.

## He Cheats Because He's Influenced By His Friends

Does he choose to be with her? Yes. Is he a cheater? Yes. Is he a cheater because of the influence of his friends? No. This is "The Truth."

The questions she should ask herself are buried below her tendencies to look beyond her man to others for his faults. Because of her perception of him, she should ask herself why she wants to be in a relationship with a grown man who can't make his own decisions? She should ask herself why she would ever entrust her heart to a man who allows his friend's actions to dictate his choices? "The Finger-Pointer" needs to ask herself if she wants to spend her time babysitting a man's moral compass to keep him from falling prey to cheating? The ultimate question she needs to answer is what the pay-off is for staying with a man who cheats because he's influenced by friends? Lying to herself when answering these questions will keep her stuck with her cheating man.

# HE CHEATED BECAUSE SHE CAME AFTER HIM

Has "The Finger-Pointer" been brainwashed? He cheats, and she fixes her gaze on the woman as the villain. When sex scandals make the news, they scrutinize the woman for her involvement. It exploits her past to assist with finding evidence to validate the character assignation that will follow. Her name is forever remembered and associated with the scandal. Not necessarily the same for the man, after all, "a man will be a man."

When "The Finger-Pointer" uses this belief as a coping mechanism, her man gets a pass for "just being a man." She believes he wouldn't have cheated unless the other woman pursued him first. This belief is unwavering, although her man took off his clothes to lay down with the woman all on his own. She must believe that the other woman had such a powerful allure that her man was spellbound and rendered incapable of thinking. Additionally, she believes that this woman made her man abandoned his values and better judgment to cheat. She would rather give the other woman all of this power than admit her man chose to cheat. He is, after all, a cheater.

She is quick to attack the other woman, and her man is more than happy to allow her to delude herself. He doesn't care where the blame is placed as long as it's not on him. As the case against the other woman develops, her cheating man gives a stellar performance as the victim of circumstances. "The Finger-Pointer" will say things like, "that tramp knew my man was in a relationship, so she had no business going after him." Hello! Her man, not the other woman, was the one who was in the relationship and therefore owed "The Finger-Pointer" his loyalty. The finger is definitely pointing in the wrong direction.

As long as she places the blame for his cheating on the other woman, she gets to stay stuck with her victim of a man. She will chastise him for not being firm enough, for allowing the other woman to control him, and for not considering the damage his cheating would cause. Nonetheless, she will not hold him accountable for his actions. In true victim mode, he will confess to feeling neglected by her, needing someone to talk to, and missing the excitement of feeling wanted. Wait a minute, did "The Finger-Pointer's" man just point the finger at her for his cheating? He sure did. He pretty much told her that if she had been giving him the attention, time, and affection that he needed, he would not have felt the need to cheat.

Let's just spin this victim mode through the full cycle. Her cheating man, who she has made into a victim, is more than eager to allow her and the other woman to take the blame for his cheating. As his defense for cheating, he will use how caring and available the other woman was while "The Finger-Pointer" hasn't been there for him lately. He may say that the other woman was his friend, and she pulled him in with her attentive nature. He may even say that the other woman made him feel wanted. It looks like what he is saying is, "The Finger-Pointer" set him up to cheat, and the other woman pulled him in to cheat. He claims no responsibility for his selfish cheating.

"The Finger-Pointer" is completely fixated on the other woman as the blame for her man's cheating, and she totally misses it when he places the blame on her. She misses her man's manipulative plot to start a competition between the two of them. Since he told her that his cheating resulted from neglect, he now expects her to put him on a pedestal for him to remain faithful. Since he put her on blast, she should now be available when he wants attention and willing to meet his every desire. She doesn't realize that she has just been elected to be the responsible party for any cheating that takes place from here on out now that she knows what it will take for her man to not cheat.

I have always found it interesting how cheating men, who are in the wrong, have been able to manipulate women into working to redeem themselves. He will have two women busy tearing one another down, jockeying for his attention and giving him his every desire. You might as well say they have given him a pass to play the field now that they know about one another. "The Finger-Pointer" believes the other woman should have kept her panties on because "a man will be a man." Because she believes that women should respect themselves, she feels that the other woman is nothing but a slut who cannot

## He Cheated Because She Came After Him

get her own man. That is why her man is not guilty; he cheated because she came after him.

The Truth is, she doesn't want to face the reality that her man cheated because "he" decided to cheat. She doesn't want to accept the reality that he continues to cheat because he wants to cheat, can cheat, and feels entitled to cheat. The Truth is, her man was fully aware of what was building between him and the other woman, and probably was the spark behind the fire. There were dozens of ways that he could have gotten his needs met, and plenty of appropriate people to occupy his time. The Truth is, her man consciously filled whatever void he might have felt with sex from another woman.

He might have said she was just a friend, so does he sleep with all of his friends? Is an affair the only way that he knows how to get his needs met? Is he incapable of setting healthy boundaries that will support him being in a committed, monogamous relationship? Is he even interested in being in a committed, monogamous relationship? Does he not know the difference between appropriate and inappropriate behavior? Answering these questions will help her point that finger in the right direction.

Even if the other woman came after him, her man could have stopped that train before it pulled into the station. Have you ever watched a train approaching from a distance, preparing to stop? It's a gradual process. At first glance, it looks to be far in the distance. You see a faint light; you hear a faint whistle, and that lets you know the train is approaching. The Truth is, her man saw the affair approaching long before he cheated. The signs of sexual attraction were there in the distance, just like the lights and whistles from an approaching train. He chose not to switch tracks or pump breaks to stay faithful.

When a train is approaching, the closer it gets, the less time you have to get out of its way. The speed is intimidating, but if you act with intention, there is still time to get to safety. "The Finger-Pointer's" man saw the sexual tension picking up speed, and he had time to get out of the situation. He felt the intensity of desire increasing and rode it out until it resulted in him cheating. The other woman is not to blame; he is responsible for his own decisions and actions. The Truth is, her man will be who he is, and cheating will always be a factor in their relationship as long as she continues to point the finger in the wrong direction. As long as the finger is pointed at the other woman for coming after her man, he will never have to reassess his choices. There will be no need for him to change, and she will remain stuck with a cheater.

The Truth is, cheating is acceptable in her man's value system. All men like attention and find it flattering to know that women find them attractive. There is nothing wrong with that. A little innocent flirting can be healthy for a relationship as long as they cross no lines. If her man were not a cheater, the advances from the other woman would have been a nice ego stroke and nothing else. If he were not a cheater, he would feel remorse for his actions, and would not feel comfortable allowing the women to be held responsible for his choices. A man who stands back and allows the finger to point in the opposite direction has no intentions of changing. The Truth is, "The Finger-Pointer" enables her man to continue to be the cheater he is by refusing to see his true character, and that will keep her stuck.

# HE CHEATED BECAUSE I \_\_\_\_\_
## (FILL IN THE BLANK)

    I really don't know which is worse, blaming someone else for your man's cheating or blaming yourself. At any rate, the finger continues to point in the wrong direction. Just as her man allowed her to blame the other woman for his cheating, he will also step aside while "The Finger-Pointer" blames herself. She is a cheater's dream come true.

    He cheated because _____. There is no shortage of reasons that her man won't allow her to own as the cause of his cheating. Whether he fills in the blank, or she manufactures her inventory of shortcomings, he will be more than happy to allow her to take full credit for causing him to cheat. "The Finger-Pointer" has lied to herself and believes that her man's cheating ways are in direct response to _____.

    All it would take is a little more thinking and a little less blaming to put this lie to rest. If her actions had the power to control her man's behaviors, why hasn't it worked in the reverse? Why hasn't she been able to nullify his cheating with her actions in the same way she believes that her actions cause him to cheat? If she would allow her wheels to spin in this direction, then she may have a chance of ending her self-deception. She did not cause him to cheat, she cannot control his cheating, and she cannot cure his cheating DNA. His choices and behaviors are all his own, and "The Finger-Pointer" is lying to herself by believing that "He Cheated Because I _____."

    Some would categorize habitual cheating as a form of emotional abuse, and just like other forms of abuse, we meet it with a measure of denial. The denial here is the fact that "The Finger-Pointer" will not acknowledge that her man is solely responsible for his decision to cheat. Her denial won't allow her to believe that his cheating is not a reaction to what she does or doesn't do for or to him. Denial has a blinding effect on

## The Truth About The Lies

most, and it has blinded her to the role of intention in her man's decisions. Cheating occurs because of intention, intention occurs because of thoughts, thoughts occur because of beliefs, and beliefs show a person's character. Her man's intention to cheat directly results from his character and his actions should not be directly linked to what she has or has not done.

It is not that she hasn't set boundaries with her man. However, when she catches him cheating, and he tells her he did so because she _____, her boundaries get blurred. Her man uses manipulation to attribute the cheating in the relationship to her actions and not his choice. His ability to distract her with her "failure" opens the door for him to point the finger of blame towards her. Now, "The Finger-Pointer" is accustomed to many things but not failure. She will not accept failure, so she gets busy trying to identify exactly what she has done to make her man cheat.

The problem with this means of coping is the words that fill in the blank will keep on changing. He cheated because I <u>wasn't affectionate enough</u>; I <u>didn't make him feel like a man</u>; I <u>was never there</u>; I <u>didn't like his friends</u>; I <u>didn't support him</u>; I <u>didn't initiate sex enough</u>, I _____ (you fill in the blank). Each time her man cheats, the blank will change. Because there is no shortage of reasons that he will cheat, there is also no shortage of blame for what she did or didn't do that caused his cheating. Once she fills one blank, another reason will pop up causing his next affair. She can never eliminate the blank and will become very good at filling it in any time her man hasn't already done so.

The Truth is, what is on the inside eventually shows up on the outside. Let's just say "The Finger-Pointer's" actions contributed to her man's decision to seek an affair. Then, he goes out intending to have an affair because of what she is or isn't doing. He chooses to cheat and then sets the scene. Never once did he divert from his intention to cheat. Why, because his nature is to cheat. He intended to cheat, set out to cheat, and cheated because of what was brewing inside of him. The Truth is, her actions might have been the spark that ignited the thought to cheat, but his intentions were fueled solely by what is inside of him.

"The Finger-Pointer" never realizes she is being jerked around like a puppet with her man acting as the puppeteer. He gets to keep cheating because he claims that her attempts to fix

## He Cheated Because I _____ (Fill In The Blank)

what is in the blank are too little or too much, too late or too soon. Her busyness of filling in the blank to avoid facing failure leads to her failure to face reality. The Truth is, she cannot win at this game, and it is truly a game. It defeats her before she gets started because he does not intend to stop the cheating. All of her efforts to correct what is in the blank act to enable her cheating man to continue to be who he is, a cheater by nature, not by prompting.

What she needs to do is point that finger in the right direction and stop contributing to the delinquency of a cheater. The Truth is, if his default action is always to cheat, then he is a cheater. He cheats because of his emotional immaturity and inability to find an appropriate means of getting his needs met. He cheats because he takes his affections outside of the relationship, and he gives it to another woman while "The Finger-Pointer" is busy trying to fix things. If she would stop lying to herself, she could see that her man's choices benefit him only, and her attempts to fix what she puts in the blank will not stop his cheating.

When "The Finger-Pointer" stops lying to herself, she can admit that she would rather be with a man who doesn't cheat because of who he is and not because of what she does to stop him from cheating. She will get unstuck when she finally accepts that her work will never be done, and therefore she stops filling in the blank. When she is ready to stop lying to herself, she will be able to admit her only failure is in trying to alter his character by what she does, hoping to reset his default to commitment not cheating. "The Finger-Pointer" will always be fearful that her man will cheat again without fear of losing her. Why, because she continues to lie to herself and believes that "He Cheated Because I _____." This keeps her stuck.

# PART 4

# LIES

# "THE DREAMER"

# TELLS HERSELF

# HE'LL CHANGE AFTER WE GET MARRIED

Despite broken promises, half-truths, inconsistencies, and indiscretions, "The Dreamer" and her man have weathered the storms of infidelity. Her ability to sacrifice and forgive has assisted her with the ability to tie a knot at the end of the rope when she didn't think she could hold on any longer. She tells herself that her man cheats because of his bachelor mentality, and after they get married, he will change. She feels she has earned the right to the title of "Mrs." and intends for him to put a ring on it.

Has she ever caught her man cheating? Yes, he has been caught cheating. Has her man changed since he was first caught cheating? If you count the fact that he has gotten better at controlling his wandering eye, controlling the urge to flirt, and keeping his commitments, then on the surface one might say that he has changed. His mentality has not changed, but he is better at controlling his behavior. No matter what, she still wants to become his wife. She sees potential, and she believes marriage will help him complete the change that he has started.

Although changes are noted, he hasn't changed enough to provide her with the sense of security she seeks in a husband. He hasn't changed enough to increase her level of trust in him. He also hasn't changed enough to give her the satisfaction of being able to say she believes he has her best interest at heart. Despite his character flaws, she sees potential in the ultimate hope that he will outgrow the temptation to cheat. She believes marriage will help him turn into the right person for her because she believes that marriage changes people and things.

In her world, there is always hope. Even though she has to defer her dream until his change comes, she is still eager to be the "Mrs." right now. She believes once they tie the knot he will settle into the married life and stop cheating. She believes marriage will help him grow up and become serious about the relationship. In her version of reality, her man will profess to God and all their loved ones, that he will love her and forsake all others. Then, magically after he says "I Do," he will change because he is now married.

Many hopeful dreamers have fallen prey to this lie and believe that a piece of paper has the spellbinding power to change a cheater into an honest man. She has stumbled into a zone where she doesn't realize that she's no longer living in reality. Just like Dorothy in the Wizard of Oz, whose dream felt so real she thought it was happening, "The Dreamer" has slipped into a state of oblivion where her man will change after they get married. All she has to do is get him to propose, and all will be well. In the *"marriage is a cure for cheating fantasy,"* "The Dreamer" believes her man will lie to her, but not to God.

Even though she knows that her man is a cheater, she believes he possesses spiritual values that won't allow him to say "I Do" and then cheat. Is marriage going to flip a switch on his value system because right now he values cheating over monogamy? Right now, his value system is set on pleasure and not principle. "The Dreamer" believes that marriage will change all that. He might be a cheater as a single man, but he won't dare commit adultery because of his spiritual values. This is the stuff that dreams are made of!

The Truth is, an important factor in having a successful marriage is choosing the right person. You cannot depend on the power of the institution of marriage alone to change a person into someone they have never been. A successful marriage is possible when two people commit to the principles that govern the institution of marriage, not when two people applying for a license and saying, "I Do." Marriage is a mindset, a commitment, a covenant, and a union. The mindset is the ideals and attitudes with which a person approaches a situation. The commitment is the act of binding yourself to a course of action, while the covenant is an agreement between the two to engage in or refrain from a specific action. Finally, the union is the oneness created by bonding or being undivided.

In "The Dreamer's" world, she disregards the above for the illusion of "potential." She approaches marriage as if it were a remedy, a transformer, or a miracle to stop cheating. A remedy will restore something to the proper condition or fix it. To transform means to change in nature or character, and a miracle is when an amazing and improbable event occurs. In

## He'll Change After We Get Married

her fantasy world, marriage will restore her cheating man to the proper mode of being faithful. Marriage will fix his thinking so that it reforms his character into that of a faithful man. As her man recites his marital vows, a miracle will take place and a transformation will result instantly. The improbable will have taken place and he will walk out of the church a changed man.

Since she sees him as a man who could be influenced by his spiritual beliefs, she would also see him as one to honor a legal obligation. After all, marriage is a legal contract with a license and a set of expectations. Because it is a contract, she believes the words "I Do" will legally bind him to her expected terms. Her expectations are those of the traditional marriage where the spouses will respect, honor, and cherish one another. She expects to be a top priority in his life and expects him to have her best interest at heart at all times. "The Dreamer" expects their marital bed to be undefiled by infidelity, despite her man's history of being a cheater.

With the lie, "He'll Change After We Get Married," she is marrying the vows and expectations instead of the man. She ignores the reality of her man's past having any part in the conditions of the marriage. Her belief in marriage as a remedy, transformer, or miracle worker has her eyes fixed on the potential instead of the likely future. She did not factor in the truth that the best chance at a healthy marriage comes from marrying the person who is right for her. The right person meaning, one who shares her visions, expectations, values, and boundaries. Starting with a man who is ready to enter and honor a marital covenant is always a primer for success.

Waiting until after the marriage for her partner to change is like waiting for a cake to finish baking after taking it out of the oven. When the cake comes out of the oven at the right time, it will be done inside and out and make for a delightful treat. Take it out before it's done, and you end up with a cake that looks good on the outside but is a mess on the inside. That's what she will get if she continues lying to herself about her man changing after marriage. When done at the right time, the man will have the right mindset for marriage and commitment. Why not simply wait for the change to occur before the marriage?

The Truth is, after marriage, "The Dreamer" will either realize she's been in a trance and finally wake up to the truth, or her illusions will turn into delusions. Illusions, by definition, are erroneous perceptions of reality. Delusions, on the other hand, are beliefs with strong convictions despite superior evidence to the contrary. If she awakens, the illusions will give way to reality and she will have to deal with the ugly truth. Once the delusions set in, there is little to no chance of her releasing the belief that her man will change after marriage. The dream will turn into a nightmare because there is no evidence to suggest that her man has adopted a new mindset and is ready to change after marriage.

The Truth is, a changed mindset is the only thing that will lead to change after marriage. A changed mindset differs greatly from a man thinking that he "might as well marry her because she's a good woman." A changed mindset is not one that holds firm to the thought that "marriage will not change me." A man who has cheated in the past, but decides that he is ready to settle down with one woman might lead to lasting change, but the proof will have to be in the commitment. His thoughts would be more like, "I'm ready to put in the effort to make this marriage work," or "I'm ready to be the man that my woman deserves." Her man has not uttered nor shown anything that remotely sounds like or looks like these are his thoughts. She should never marry potential because potential might never materialize into the dream, and that will keep her stuck with a cheater.

# HE'LL CHANGE AFTER WE HAVE A CHILD

Whether married or single, after being in a relationship for some time without a solid commitment, "The Dreamer" contemplates ideas of what they need to strengthen their bond. She has catered to his needs and made every effort to show her man that he is a top priority in her life. It doesn't feel as though the feeling is mutual. She can't shake the nagging sense of detachment and superficiality in the level of their bond, and she feels something has to be added to the equation for him to change.

If already married, the original misconception was that her cheating man would change after they said, "I Do." By now, she has been married long enough to realize the potential for change she believed possible is not materializing. Her man has entered the institution of marriage without committing to the traditional rules and expectations she thought would follow. Remember, in the last chapter, I said that if she does not awaken from the illusion, she would develop delusions. In her delusional world, she now shifts to the belief that her man will change after they have a child.

The "single" dreamer might feel that her man doesn't take the relationship seriously and hasn't decided he wants a solid commitment. Although he has not ended the relationship, she often questions her label; who is she to him, and what are they doing? She has tried all that she can to elevate her status to a higher identifiable level with no success. Naively, she believes that having a child will help him to see her and experience the relationship differently. In her dream, having a child will reel him in and secure her place in his life.

The "single" dreamer has attributed her man's lack of commitment to emotional immaturity. She believes that having a child will magically cause him to mature, and with maturity comes commitment. In her dreams, he will share the pregnancy

## The Truth About The Lies

experience, and as the baby grows in her belly, the relationship bond will deepen. She believes with each passing month his commitment to her will be increasing. As he prepares for the responsibilities of fatherhood, he will lose all motivation for being with another woman because now they have a child.

Married or single, "The Dreamer" continues to lie to herself about his potential. She believes that he will surely change after they have a child because that will move them from *coupledom* to becoming a family. She has witnessed how moved he was by friends becoming fathers. She has grazed the subject of them having a child, and he agrees that when the time is right, they will. According to "The Dreamer" now is as good a time as any, and all he needs to help him change is the title of "father." They will now earn the label "family," and he will honor that label even though he has not chosen to honor a commitment to being faithful.

The dream goes something like this; woman gets pregnant; wayward man dotes on her; baby arrives; wayward man is so smitten by the baby he falls in love with the woman; wayward man loves his family too much to do anything to lose them; wayward man becomes the perfect "family man." Dreams don't always come true. Sometimes becoming a father shifts a man's values in the right direction. However, becoming a committed father and becoming a committed partner is not the same. She continues to believe the lie that he will commit and change after they have a child, despite his history to the contrary.

The Truth is, having a baby simply adds another role to his life, but it doesn't automatically enhance his existing role. Imagining him with their child gives her high hopes that the love she has always longed for will be hers once he is a father. She believes the love he will have for the baby will trickle down to her because he will appreciate her more for giving him a child. After all, she will be the reason that he is a daddy and that alone should give him warm and fuzzy feelings towards her. The new labels of father and family are what "The Dreamer" believes will change her man.

The Truth is, "The Dreamer" is holding on to her man because she believes they will have a better relationship after having a child. This belief is just creating another way for her to stay stuck with him. He has already proven to be a cheater, and she has already committed herself to him, hoping he will

## He'll Change After We Have A Child

eventually change. By adding a baby to the mix, she will create a commitment to her child that includes having two parents in the home. Her driving force will now be to make him share her commitment to family. She dreams of being successful and cementing her place in his life.

Here are a few tough questions she should ask herself to assist with challenging the lies she has embraced. How many men have continued cheating after having a child? How many men have had children by multiple women? How many men have left women after having children? How can a woman be emotionally secure in a relationship with a man who is committed to the child and not her? If she will honestly analyze these questions, she will find The Truth. Afterward, she can start making conscious choices based on reality and wake up from the dream of her man changing after having a child.

The Truth is, she has to embrace the fact that there are no guarantees in life. If she is lucky, he will be an active father. She can hope that he will embrace the role of father, but there is no guarantee. If single, she might often find herself home alone, wondering where he is. If married, having a child may spark change in him, or she may join the ranks of the "married single mothers." She believes that adding a child to the equation will now create a sense of family and result in commitment. Many men have stayed with women because of the child, but that does not guarantee he will be faithful. Being committed to his family and being committed to his partner are totally different things. The Truth is, "The Dreamer" is using a child to accomplish what she could not, which is to change her cheating man.

Expecting her child to accomplish what she hasn't been able to, she will unconsciously begin using the child to manipulate him into not cheating. In her delusional state, "The Dreamer" believes having a child will lead him to maturity. She will envision the child as his reason not to hang out so often, not to stay out so late, and to want to come home at night. If his actions are counter to her delusion, then the manipulation will ensue where she will make her needs the child's needs by saying things like, "your child needs daddy at home, misses daddy when he's not home, and deserves to spend more time with daddy." She will keep their child front and center in her conversations that requesting more of his time because if he is going to change, she believes it will be because of the child.

## The Truth About The Lies

The Truth is, she will hold on to her delusion with all her might because if not, she will have to face all the lies that have kept her stuck for so many years. She will have to go back to when she lied to herself after the first time he cheated. She saw his cheating, accepted it, and stayed because of "his potential." Why, because she lied to herself and believed he would change after they had a child. If married, after the "I Do's," he proved to be the same cheater he had always been. There was no change in his commitment to her, but she maintained hope in his ability to stop cheating. That's when she upped the ante and added a child to the equation as the motivation for him to stop cheating. Now that she has a child, and he has not changed, will she accept her reality, or will she simply find something else to fall back on? Getting unstuck is not possible without facing reality and releasing hope in the potential that her man will stop cheating because they have a child.

# HE'LL CHANGE AFTER WE GO TO COUNSELING

I'll be the first to admit that couples therapy is one of the most challenging modalities of counseling. You have two people who come to counseling attempting to achieve some type of change. The problem is the change the partners seek is rarely the same. Individual motives drive the couple into the counselor's office under the pretenses that they both want the change that is best for their union. Normally, what they want is for the counseling, or the counselor, to change the other partner.

Few things cut deeper than finding out that your man has cheated. Cheating is a selfish act. It leaves the woman feeling the entire relationship was built on lies. The devastation penetrates every aspect of her being and sends her on an emotional roller coaster. As she attempts to sort through the hurt, pain, and confusion, she will often suggest counseling to heal from the emotional trauma of infidelity. The world, as she knew it, has completely changed, leaving her vulnerable, shocked, and wounded to the core.

Once the initial shock wears off, if the woman stays with her cheating man, she will have many questions. She will wonder what aspects of the relationship were real. Her image of her man would have changed so much that she will question whether she ever really knew him at all. Normally, she feels like she needs him to assist her with the healing process and to bring closure to this nightmare. Here is where "The Dreamer" mentality escalates. She deludes herself into believing that bringing him to counseling will cause him to become honest, insightful, and thoughtful; a man who will provide her with the comfort and security needed to heal.

She believes bringing her cheating man to counseling will answer all of her questions, he will gain insight into why he cheats, they will share their way to clarity, and he will change. Only in her dreams will this happen immediately following an affair. She has to realize that this is still the man who was able to cheat, lie, and deceive. No change has taken place other than the fact that she now knows he has cheated again. He agreed to take part in counseling because he cares about her wellbeing, but caring is not enough to change his character. Nonetheless, she expects total honesty and full disclosure about all of his dirt. She expects him to understand how badly the cheating hurt her, and to be ready to conform to all of her expectations. With expectations like this, counseling often results in more anger, frustration, and disappointment.

Typically, cheating causes the woman to enter counseling feeling devastated, confused, used, humiliated, and betrayed. It's as if she was cut wide open and gutted because of the emptiness she feels. Nothing can be more confusing for the woman than trying to understand how the man who said that he loved her could cheat. For counseling to do what "The Dreamer" wants it to, her man would have to know why he initially cheated, why he continues to cheat, why he didn't think that cheating was wrong, and how he could love her and cheat simultaneously. He would have to want to change. He has cheated before, and therefore, she feels this time around counseling will help them decode the mystery of his cheating and eliminate the problem.

Because she will become insecure in her ability to keep him, self-doubt causes anxiety and sleepless nights. Because he cheated, she wonders if she is desirable enough, good enough, exciting enough, pretty enough, and simply enough for him. Her mind will run wild with questions about him and the other woman. *"Who was she? Do I know her/does she know me? When did it start/is it over? How long did it last? How many times did they have sex? When/where did they have sex? Where/how did he meet her?"* and the ultimate *"Does he love her?"* are the questions that flood in like a tidal wave. In her dreams, counseling will allow her to get all the answers to the questions that keep her up at night.

What I've often experienced while working with "The Dreamer" is the expectation of counseling working a miracle. Counseling will be like hypnosis and will evoke insight and remorse in the cheater. She envisions him having an awakening and seeing the error of his ways. Then, there will be a spiritual transformation, and he will now denounce his bad habits. Next, he will commit to changes that will lead to her heart's desires.

# He'll Change After We Go To Counseling

In her dream, her man will change once they go to counseling.

"The Dreamer" is typically naturally emotional. She finds comfort in talking things through, expressing her feelings, and feeling understood. That's why a long heart-to-heart with a girlfriend can bring her comfort and clarity after being betrayed. In her dreams, counseling is super-charged emotional therapy that will challenge the cheater's mindset by extracting out all the poisonous thoughts and beliefs that led to his promiscuous ways. She expects counseling to restructure his perceptions of right and wrong by awakening his conscience, which will enable him to feel guilt and shame. She believes the heightened consciousness and restructured perception he will develop from going to counseling will act as venom to his past poisonous ways of thinking. In this dream, he will definitely change once they go to counseling.

Her goals for counseling are to confront her man about his cheating, validate her opinions, confirm her suspicions, and ultimately to change him. She hopes that counseling will hypnotically pull the truth out of him, just like she's seen it done in the movies. The counselor's job is to change her man. Her cheating man's goal is to go to a few counseling sessions simply to ease the tension. He hopes that the mere act of agreeing to go to counseling will increase her trust in him. He expects the counselor to help them put the past behind them ASAP and move into the future, never to revisit the subject of his cheating.

There's a major problem here because "The Dreamer" expects counseling to change her man. Women generally find comfort in talking things out to understanding why things happen. Men don't. She believes that counseling will turn him into an accountable adult ready to take responsibility for his actions. Resulting from his newfound ability to be accountable, she expects him to grow into a changed man. After counseling, she expects him to make lifestyle changes and erase cheating from his system. This expectation is unrealistic and more likely to happen in her dreams. What is more likely to happen is, her cheating man will grow tired of answering the same questions repeatedly. He'll tell her she is stuck in the details and that there is no way for them to move on if she keeps dwelling on the past.

The Truth is, "The Dreamer" is stuck in the details. She has a razor-sharp focus on the details of his cheating and seeks more answers and confessions through counseling. She dreams that the counseling sessions will assist her by having a third-party to rephrase her previous questions until she hears the answers she wants to hear, get answers to the questions she was afraid to ask, and challenge all inconsistencies in details she has gathered from her cheating man. Because of her focus, she will never get what she wants from counseling, because counseling never results in change when used as a weapon. Counseling will comprise questioning and re-questioning, preaching and moralizing, and threats of consequences and repercussions. The chances of him gaining any insight, being enlightened, or having an "ah-ha" moment that could lead to change will be thwarted by his need to stay on guard and plan a defense for the ambush that awaits him each time he enters counseling.

Another aspect of The Truth is counseling rarely results in *a cheater* changing, but it will lead to a change with *a man who has cheated.* It is very easy to distinguish which one you are in a relationship with if you pay attention. For a *man who has cheated,* going to counseling will result in drastically different dynamics than that of *a cheater* going to counseling. First, *a man who has cheated* is not simply going to counseling, he is taking part in the process of change with his woman. *A cheater* is simply going to counseling with his woman because she thinks it will be helpful. "The Dreamer" needs to accept that she is with *a cheater* and not *a man who has cheated,* since this is not the first time that her man cheated. The Truth is, coming to counseling with a cheater expecting lasting change is a setup for failure and disappointment.

As said before, the experience is very different with *a cheater* versus *a man who has cheated. A man who has cheated* believes that he can benefit from counseling and he wants to gain a deeper understanding of why he cheated. He is truly ashamed of his actions and feels he had no justification to cheat. *A cheater* bears no shame in the fact that he cheated, will use the counseling to point out flaws in his woman and the relationship to justify his cheating, and doesn't see any benefit in sitting down with a stranger to talk about what he and she have already discussed. *A man who has cheated* and *a cheater* will not get the same thing out of counseling because they are not wired in the same way for change. *A man who has cheated* will engage in counseling, but *a cheater* will endure counseling.

## He'll Change After We Go To Counseling

*A man who has cheated* is sensitive to his woman's feelings and is truly sorry for having put her through this pain. Therefore, willing to take full responsibility for his actions, answer all of her questions, and do whatever it takes to regain her trust. *A cheater* is frustrated by his woman's pain and is tired of answering the same questions repeatedly. He feels that counseling is the reason his woman cannot trust him because she keeps harping on the same old details instead of trying to move on. *A man who has cheated* is taking part in counseling for personal growth and to repair his relationship. He will go to counseling for as long as it takes his woman to feel secure in their relationship. *A cheater* is going to counseling for his woman so she can get over his cheating. She is the one who needs to grow, not him, and she'd better do it fast because he has no intention of going to counseling forever. While *a man who has cheated* sees counseling as a solution to strengthen his relationship, *a cheater* sees it as a duty that will lead to a quick fix to moving on.

"The Dreamer" needs to stop lying to herself and accept the fact that she is with a cheater, not a man who has cheated. Most dreamers will not accept the fact that their cheaters might not ever change. The Truth is, cheaters are normally more interested in focusing on the woman changing when they come to counseling by pointing out what she was not doing, what she wasn't giving him, and what she needs to do differently to make him stop cheating. "The Dreamer" is lost in details while in counseling and cannot connect the dots that draw a clear picture of her man's inability to see his cheating as a problem. His frustration, irritation, and defensiveness should be the red flags that show his unwillingness to change. She fails to realize the only change her man is interested in is changing the subject from what he has done to what she caused him to do. She doesn't realize that his ability to justify his actions based on what he wasn't getting is a sign he will continue to cheat. She can never give him everything he "thinks" he needs. The Truth is, counseling will not change him. She will have to accept reality; she will continue to get what she currently has in her relationship with him.

The Truth is, "The Dreamer" will never get closure from going to counseling with her cheating man. The answers he throws out will never satisfy her. His rationale and logic for why he did what he did will never make sense to her, and she will never understand how he could love her and cheat. Her primary reason for dragging him into counseling is to make him fully understand the many ways she felt hurt, degraded, betrayed, and disrespected. Either she comes into counseling wearing a halo to signify her righteousness, or an emotional body cast to show him how badly the cheating has wounded her to the core. She wants the counseling to accomplish what she hasn't been able to since she first found out about his cheating. He wants the counseling to get her off his back.

Neither of them will get what they want from counseling, and they will work against each other's goals. When counseling is used as a weapon, instead of a resource for growth, it never works. "The Dreamer" keeps lying to herself and expecting that eventually she and her man will use the counseling to bond. She wants to talk about what lead to them disconnecting and what lead to him straying. She expects that they will work together to find solutions to their problems, which will cause them to reconnect. "The Dreamer" hopes that her man will become vested in doing whatever it takes to help her heal. She keeps hope alive by continuing to drag her man into the counselor's office.

The cheater often discontinues counseling prematurely. Counseling is considered a waste of time, and he blames it for keeping the negativity active. He doesn't see how talking about his dirt will help to fix anything and refuses to sit there while she makes him look bad. Her man will eventually blame the counselor for keeping them stuck and keeping her angry. He will even scapegoat the counseling for making the relationship worse. There is no desire to change, with or without counseling.

The next time "The Dreamer's" man cheats, and he will cheat again, he will blame the counseling. He will maintain that the counseling did nothing but keep the focus on their problems. He will refuse to acknowledge the fact that he created the problems that lead to the need for counseling. It will not be an option for him to admit his defensiveness and unwillingness to continue to answer questions, and constantly telling her she needed to get over it, caused her anger. He will not admit the relationship got worse because he was not willing to change, and she will attempt to pull him back into counseling believing change will come.

The Truth is, she should go to counseling alone instead of dragging him along. Better use of her time would be to seek counseling to understand herself, examine her wants, and be honest about what her man can deliver. She should go to counseling for personal growth and heal the parts of her that keep her stuck with her cheating man. She should seek to understand why she stays with him and why she continues to lie to herself about what she thinks counseling will accomplish. "The Dreamer" should consider counseling to assist with restructuring her distorted beliefs about him changing and regaining her confidence to make decisions based on who he is currently instead of who she thinks he has the potential to become. She should be the one who changes after she goes to counseling by accepting the fact that she is in a relationship with a cheater who may never change. Until then, the lies will keep her stuck with her cheating man.

# HE'LL CHANGE AFTER HE RECOMMITS TO THE CHURCH

*The family that prays together stays together.* If there is one thing believed to have the ability to change a person, it's "the church." Revelation, repentance, and transformation are all possible if "The Dreamer" can get her cheating man to recommit himself to the church. In her dreams, all the cheater has to do is attend weekly, listen intently, and apply the word to his sinful life. With this equation, change is certain. He said he grew up in the church, and he has attended sparingly with her, so now all she has to do is lead the way.

"The Dreamer" sees the church as a metaphorical glue that keeps things intact. She believes if couples attend church together, it will enhance their chances of developing a healthy bond. For her, attending church together is symbolic of being on one accord, and of one mind. She believes that regular church attendance is a significant factor of her man staying morally attuned to right and wrong. If only she can get him out of bed on Sunday morning, get him to put off the yard work, or get him to record the game, she can then drag him to the church for his weekly dose of cleansing.

Her belief that if he recommits to the church, he will change, is not all together delusional. What would make it delusional is her believing that a building and a few sermons have the mystical power to change her man. She knows that the church is where you take your problems and lay them on the altar. The church is where sins are confessed and we seek forgiveness. Therefore, she has strong faith in the possibility of him changing once he recommits to the church.

She is not bearing in mind that the simple act of going into the church does not mean that he will change. She has not taken into consideration her man would first have to want to change, seek change, and feel change is necessary before any change will occur. The argument for her strong faith is that

God can do anything. Once again, she is leaving out a key component of this belief; God, who can do anything, gave us all free will to choose. Change comes from within, and I do not mean from within a building.

The devastation caused by cheating men has driven many women to their knees. It has provoked even more women to seek counsel from their pastors. She knows her man has to want to change, but she believes this is different. This is God's house, a sanctuary, a holy place where miracles can happen. This is "the church," so if she can get her cheating man to recommit to the church, he will change.

Belief in the idea of him changing after he recommits to the church leads to an obsessive routine of church attendance. If he misses a church service, she will buy the recording, so he doesn't skip a beat. If her man doesn't want to attend bible study, she will stay home with him and the two of them will have a study session. Her anxiety rises with each missed church service and decreases in direct proportion to the number of services he attends. It's as if she believes that the amount of change directly correlates to the number of services that her cheating man attends.

Imagine her surprise when he slacks off from her mandatory church attendance. After all, the average cheater only agrees to attend church with his woman because she presented an ultimatum or necessary activity for continuing in the relationship. The *cheater* knows how strong his woman's faith is, so he figures he'll score brownie points by complying with her demands about church attendance until the dust settles. Her delusional belief in him changing because of church attendance obstructed her view of his gradual resistance to going to church. She was taken aback when her man reverted to his old Sunday routine of staying home while she attended church. As said before, change happens from within.

What does she do now that recommitting to the church has run a short-lived course? When she attends church without him, she is distracted by his absence and can hardly follow the sermon. Now and again, the pastor will say something that grabs her attention, and she writes it down so she can "preach at" him. As soon as she hits the church parking lot, she is on the phone calling him to chastise him for not attending church. Not to worry, she purchased the CD with plans to leave it in his CD player so her backsliding, cheating man will hear it as soon

## He'll Change After He Recommits To The Church

as he starts his car. She is determined to lead him down the path of recommitting to the church.

The obsessive nature of her belief in the necessity of church attendance, to promote change, spirals out of control. If he won't attend church, she will bring the church to him. Now, on Sunday mornings, she stays home to supervise his spiritual growth. Thanks to modern technology, "The Dreamer" has other resources. She finds church services on television and has every set in the house turned to the designated channel to broadcast the programs. She thinks this might be an even better option since programs will broadcast from sunup to sundown. Surely, he will not deny God by changing the channel. I have to wonder what is happening to her commitment to the church amid trying to make him recommit?

The popular saying, *"You can take the horse to the water, but you can't make him drink,"* reigns supreme. As "The Dreamer" supervises her cheating man's church activities, she doesn't notice any signs of transformation in his thinking and behaviors, but it does not defeat her. If she can't get him to go to church, she will get those who go to church to come to him. You got it; she plans to arrange for a series of spiritual play dates with men from the church. She will strategize and plot until she has created the perfect setup for these men to assist her with getting her cheating man to recommit to the church. All they have to do is share their past failures and current transformations to convince her man of the blessings that await him once he recommits to the church.

"The Dreamer" has put a lot of time and energy into getting her man to recommit to the church in hopes that he will change his cheating ways. At some point, she will have to stop lying to herself. The Truth is, attending church has not changed him at all. She has to re-evaluate her belief in the power of church attendance and church members to change him. She will have to admit The Truth; her man is not interested in changing, therefore will not change until he decides a change is necessary. Why should he change? Look at all the time and attention he has gotten from her for his inappropriate behavior. As long as he allows her to try to fix him, he gets to stay flawed and keep her at the same time.

The Truth is, she is not the captain of her man's spiritual development, and growth is the product of spiritual awakening. This differs from the religious doctrine that most get from church attendance. Religious doctrine is instructional and comes with a list of commands and abominations. Spiritual development happens more intimately. Most believe divine intervention precedes spiritual awakening and "The Dreamer's" interference has not been divine at all. All of her manipulations have caused obsessive behaviors, and her man still has not changed. If he wasn't committed to the church before he cheated, and she made it mandatory, then there was never any hope of sincere and lasting change.

The Truth is, if being connected to a church could nullify the urge to cheat, we wouldn't have any stories in the news about preachers who have cheated. We would have no womanizing pastors if the church could erase the urge to cheat. If the man delivering the sermon is still prone to cheat, what makes "The Dreamer" believes that her man will change because he commits to the church? What he needs to commit to is change, and that's the only commitment that will lead to her man being faithful.

Not to discredit the role of the church, and the power of attendance, because it could lead to change for those who are true seekers. What church attendance might do to a cheater is provoke guilt and shame, or the sermon could touch him emotionally. This could be the beginning of him contemplating change. Church attendance might even provoke remorse for past actions, but it's not likely to prevent future cheating unless he is seeking change. Thinking about change, preparing to change, and actually changing are all separate phases in the process of change. If "The Dreamer" wants to get unstuck, she should ask herself if her cheating man appears to be in either of these phases. She should not mistake church attendance as a panacea for change. That will simply keep her stuck with a cheating man who attends church.

# PART 5

# LIES

# "THE HELPLESS"

## TELLS HERSELF

# HE'S ALL I GOT /
# I DON'T WANT TO LOSE HIM

One of the most devastating hurts a woman experiences is when she finds out the man she is committed to is cheating. The realization results in indescribable heartache, surreal pain, and incomprehensible shock that she prays will all just go away. The pain is accompanied by all-consuming waves of emotion that render most women helpless to cope effectively. Because the hurt is too much for some to endure, they would rather cling to the source of their pain by trying to mend the wounds rather than tearing completely away and leaving a gaping hole. It's like a person who has stepped on a nail deeply piercing their flesh, but they don't want anyone to touch it. Yes, the pain is agonizing, but pulling the nail out will subject them to more excruciating pain than they can handle. This is how "The Helpless" is born.

The lie that her cheating man is all that she has creates an emotional trap for "The Helpless." This lie is magnified by the drama she created in her mind, and in her life, to avoid the truth. The result of continuously compromising, sacrificing, and abandoning her values, boundaries, and needs is, she has lost herself in her man's world. She has given away so much of herself that it feels like he is all she has, and she is trying desperately not to lose him.

I have worked with countless women who share this belief when confronted with infidelity. They started neglecting and abandoning friendships, family, and hobbies to intercept their man's opportunities to cheat. Each time he cheated, "The Helpless" abandoned more of her core values, beliefs, and needs to stay in the relationship. Her sense of helplessness is masked by her ability to over-function trying to safeguard the relationship from being ravaged by his indiscretions. Like anything that weakens after experiencing repeated pressure, cheating has beaten her down emotionally. "The Helpless" feels like he is all she has because she has given up everything to keep him.

"He's all I've got/I don't want to lose him," interpreted is, "I have abandoned myself and no longer know who I am." She has relinquished far too much of her identity in this relationship. Her life is unbalanced, and she has allowed her cheating man to dominate the core of her existence. He has become her primary focus, his needs have become her primary responsibility, and pleasing him has become her primary goal in life. When did this happen? How did this happen? Why did this happen? It started the first time he cheated, and she stayed. She thought she could make things better, different, or right by giving more and more of herself.

The woman who stays with her man after he cheats generally develops a common belief pattern. A layer of her self-confidence is stripped away, causing her to struggle to maintain a healthy self-image and self-esteem. She doubts her worth and questions who she is and what she means to him. When doubt consumes her thoughts, she will look to him to redefine her worth, validate who she is, and help restore the confidence she once possessed naturally. Because she has given him the task of reconstructing her after feeling emotionally gutted by his cheating, she has to stay with him to feel significant.

"The Helpless" looks at her choice to stay with him as a long-term investment with risks, like investing in the stock market. Just because the market crashes, it does not mean you should rush in and sell all your stock. Most financial brokers would advise investors to ride it out until the market rebounds. There are risks associated with riding out the stock market as well as staying in the relationship. The market, and the relationship, both have the potential to stabilize. Also, there is the potential the market will crash again just as there is the potential the man will cheat again. Be forewarned; you may not recoup all your losses. Choosing to stay leaves her helpless to the possibility.

On the path of attempting to prevent her cheating man from abandoning her, "The Helpless" actually starts to abandon herself. After he has cheated and she has stayed, she will throw herself into the relationship. Anxiously, she creates a list of changes necessary to safeguard the relationship from his cheating. This is where she loses balance and he becomes the bane of her existence. "The Helpless" will abandon her normal routines, hobbies, friends, and family and desperately cling to him. She avoids everything from working late to social events that don't include him because she fears where he will go and who he will entertain in her absence.

"The Helpless" has become extremely vulnerable and clingy. She has gone to the extremes of packing his lunch, taking lunch to him, or meeting him for lunch daily to prevent him from using his break to cheat. She is available for everything and anything that he wants to do and invites him to every event she attends. Her life has revolved totally around him to keep him faithful. He is all that she has because this is the world she has created.

"The Helpless" doesn't even realize she is abandoning herself while overcompensating for her man. She doesn't realize she is losing herself in the process of trying to keep him. She continues to invest all her time, energy, and emotion into their relationship. He enjoys playing cards, so she plays with him. He goes to the club, so she tags along with him every chance that she's given. He doesn't attend church, so she stays home with him. None of this clingy activity is resulting in a stronger bond with him; it's simply her playing interference so he won't be with another woman. Sadly, this continues until she has abandoned herself totally and has become a prototype of the woman she thinks he needs for him to stay and not cheat.

After all the adjustments, compromises, and sacrifices, there's no wonder she feels he is all she has. It makes perfect sense that she doesn't want to lose him because now there is no "her" left. If all this were a true investment in the relationship's betterment, then there would be no loss. She wouldn't have been the only one making deposits. All he did was make withdrawals from her time, energy, and emotional investment while she deposited everything she had into him. If he cannot invest anything into the relationship, then she will reap no returns on her investment.

The Truth is, while "The Helpless" was telling herself that her man is all she has, she was trying to make herself all he had. She was making herself so available, so accommodating, and so valuable to him hoping he would stop cheating. She wanted him to see her as indispensable so he would never leave. Her goal is to make him see there is no other woman who could ever need or want him the way she does.

She became more vulnerable when she saw glimmers of the truth and realized she had given all that she could. She gave her all to him, and her all was not enough. Sadly, she still suspects he is cheating. To get unstuck, she has to realize there is nothing she can do to make him stop cheating and be the man that she feels she deserves. The Truth is, because she has drained herself in this relationship, she has no energy to leave and start over with someone new. Because she has lied to herself for so long about him being all she has and abandoned herself in so many ways, she feels empty. There is nothing left for her to give to a new relationship, so she feels helplessly stuck with her cheating man. He is all that she has.

Before she can begin repairs, there should be an accurate assessment of damages. If "The Helpless" would step outside the box she has created, she could see the self-inflicted wounds. An accurate assessment would show her that there were no returns on her investments; she should have withdrawn all of herself from the bankrupt relationship. Her assessment would show that she de-valued herself, disrespected herself, and disregarded herself to avoid abandonment. If she is ready for The Truth, she will assess that her investments added no value to the relationship and there was no insurance to cover the emotional damage suffered while attempting to prevent him from cheating. In the end, she is stuck with her cheating man because she abandoned herself. He wasn't *all that she had* until she made him all that she had.

# I FEEL STUCK

When a woman has labored in a less-than-desirable relationship and goes against her value system to stay with a cheating man, she loses the ability to make healthy decisions that meet her needs. The power to set and commit to her previously established boundaries weakens. She continues to reposition her boundary lines in order to stay in the relationship. Continuously straying is the key factor in feeling stuck and continuously feeling stuck leads to becoming "The Helpless." However, feeling stuck is a state of her mind, not a state of her being.

One of the most common reasons women say they stay in dead-end relationships is feeling stuck. What they mean by "feeling stuck" is having the desire to leave, but not knowing how or when to break free, end the drama, or exit with grace. Some will say they cannot afford to leave because of finances. Others won't own their power and permit themselves to leave. The majority will have a laundry list of barriers to challenge any reason they might legitimately have for leaving, which is why they feel stuck.

There are a few commonalities to how "The Helpless" came to feel stuck. Not having money, credit, energy, right, or power to leave are the most common themes women cite for feeling stuck. If she lives with her man, she possibly cannot afford what they have together, cannot split joint assets easily, or doesn't want to pay what it will cost for a place of her own. He may pay most of the bills, or they may share the expenses, which has created a comfort zone that is difficult to leave. She has probably become irresponsible or very comfortable with money and savings. Her irresponsibility might have created some blemishes on her credit that will hinder her ability to get a place of her own, while her comfort might have created a tangible lifestyle that she doesn't want to give up. She feels stuck with him for various reasons.

Moving on requires a reserve of energy and motivation to ignite action. We can generate energy and motivation from either negative or positive sources. The woman could feel fed up with her man's drama, and anger becomes her source of energy. Experiencing a spiritual awakening could motivate her to do better. Staying in a box, or a comfort zone, leads to feeling stuck because at the core she knows she is not where she should be. Fear is the most common energy and motivation blocker in the world. Fear of failure, the known, the unknown, and the new are some reasons used to create a laundry list of barriers and challenges that cause "The Helpless" to feel stuck.

She might say that she doesn't have the right to leave or the power to walk away. "The Helpless" may feel as if she owes him something. He may have been there for her during a rough patch, provided for her needs, or assisted her with achieving goals. He could have accepted her "as-is," flaws and all, with all of her insecurities. Because of this, she minimizes the weight of his emotionally draining cheating and feels as if she doesn't have the right to leave. Power comes from knowing your worth, and when a woman has endured repeated cheating, she questions the essence of her worth. She might not trust that she can make it on her own, not believe anyone else would want her, or has become so helpless she states that he won't let her leave.

All the above are the lies "The Helpless" has created that keep her stuck in an unfulfilled life and a rut with her cheating man. The reality is normally not half as complicated as the lies she has created. The worst-case scenario is usually more practical, like not being able to maintain the same lifestyle she has grown accustomed to or having to get a better job. She might have to develop another source of income to support her becoming self-sufficient. "The Helpless" might have to do what she fears, which is being alone until she finds the right man while learning to appreciate a drama-free life. All the above could be positive changes but will be considered barriers to leaving, therefore she feels stuck.

We haven't even touched on the role of her morals and beliefs. "The Helpless" feels stuck because she has too many rules. She thinks methodically, and that makes it hard to draw a straight line to what is right and wrong for her. Her ability to mix traditional morals, spiritual doctrine, social norms, and relationship trends leave her in a quandary of indecision. She feels stuck because she has lost the ability to make decisions based on what's best for her, what feels right to her, and what

## I Feel Stuck

matches her core beliefs. The moral dilemma leads her to talk with too many people, which results in more confusion. She feels stuck because she will not make her own decision based primarily on her own needs and values.

The first time she stayed after he cheated was probably for moral reasons. She believed that forgiveness was mandatory, and he deserved a second chance. Those beliefs are essential aspects of her value system, so she stayed. Forgiveness wasn't automatic, and she worked extremely hard to stay with him without judgment. Morally, she believed she was doing what was right; this did not bring her comfort and satisfaction. Her list of "shoulds" kept her bound to him while trying to honor her moral beliefs and her value system. She thought she would find satisfaction and contentment in doing the right thing. Instead, she felt stuck because of her moral obligation to forgive a man that would continue to repeat the same behaviors.

Nothing complicates the moral dilemma more than having children with your cheating man. "The Helpless" feels convicted, not only by what is right and wrong for her, but now she has to consider what is right and wrong for her children. Anxious fantasies about how the children will suffer and the negative stigma connected to raising children in a single-parent home plague her thoughts. The battle between her heart and head intensifies her indecision and renders her immobile; she is feeling stuck.

Let's decode why she feels stuck. Typically, women feel stuck because they are with someone who is not meeting their primary needs. They are generally with a man they have outgrown, and they cannot see things changing for the better. The relationship has run its course. The two of them are more like roommates or friends if they have managed to still like one another. She feels stuck because to get out of this relationship she has to be prepared for quite a few changes that she's just not ready to make. She has to be ready to change her lifestyle, become comfortable being single, and adjust to letting go of relationships she has built while with him. It's bigger than just letting him go and walking away. Major changes will follow the ending of the relationship, and she is not ready for change. Therefore, she feels stuck.

Because her feelings for him have changed, she feels stuck. They may have a roommate-style relationship if living together and are primarily bonded by bills and responsibilities. They may not feel connected any longer, but just tolerate one another. Communication patterns and interactions probably have changed from loving to cordial, from relaxed to strained, and from consistent to random. She has gotten to the point of sincerely wishing her cheating man would just leave and go be with the other women. This is not how she envisioned living her life.

To intensify the feeling of being stuck she engages in some self-defeating behaviors. Her distance, coldness, and lack of intimacy set her man up to continue to cheat. She almost gives him a license to cheat because she has grown to a point of numbness. She thinks she is being smart and guarding her heart by acting indifferent, but this only intensifies the feeling of being stuck. Now she is with a man who she doesn't want to be with, doesn't care who he is with, but because of mitigating circumstances, she won't leave. She says she is preparing to leave and will do so after she has done "so and so," but until that day arrives, she will feel stuck.

Many self-help gurus will agree that if you fight for your limitations, you get to keep them. The Truth is, she has been fighting for her limitations instead of preparing for her desires. She spends countless hours tallying up reasons and circumstances to support why she cannot leave right now. The true essence of it all is, being stuck is a way of bargaining for more time for him to get his act together, more time for her to start to love him again, and more time for him to repay her for what he's taken away. The Truth is, because of the repeated cheating "The Helpless" does not have enough ego strength to leave, to make a firm decision, or to do what is best for her. As long as she continues to generate her list of reasons she cannot leave and to replay those old tapes in her head, she will stay stuck in the relationship with her cheating man.

The Truth is, feeling stuck is a state of mind, and the circumstances are not right for leaving because of how she views them. She has made various sacrifices for her cheating man, but she is not willing to sacrifice for her own happiness and peace of mind. Leaving him will require some serious sacrifices. She may have to live with family or friends until she is prepared to live on her own. Other changes may include getting a new job, or two, that pays all her bills, renting versus buying, and giving up some luxuries that accompany the

## I Feel Stuck

current lifestyle. If there are children involved, there will be changes that will affect them directly. They may have to adjust to a new home, neighborhood, or school. Also, they will have to adjust to not seeing both parents daily and growing up in a single-parent home.

The Truth is, her life will be different, but there will be movement instead of stagnation. Everything she has considered as a problematic reason she could not leave now is simply a change that she will have to make in her life. Having to give up things is a part of growing and changing. The only limitation "The Helpless" has is the fact that she is not ready to give up anything. We are never really stuck because there is at least one other alternative. It might not be what we want, like, or desire however, the option is available. Feeling stuck is more about not embracing change than anything else. The list of reasons she cannot leave is simply a list of things that will have to change. The Truth is, she feels stuck because she is not ready to, doesn't want to, or feels like she shouldn't have to make any changes.

"The Helpless" has lied to herself about the source of feeling stuck. The Truth is, the relationship with her cheating man will never satisfy her, and she will not find peace within herself by staying with him. She is not stuck with him, and she is not stuck with the circumstances she has listed as reasons for staying. What she is stuck with is a lack of peace because of how she thinks about it all. She is stuck with the mindset of feeling stuck. "The Helpless" is stuck in a state of frustration because she cannot make a concrete decision based on facts that will lead to actions versus ruminating on her list of immobilizing limitations.

I have heard it said, "change your mind, change your life," also "actions speak louder than words." "The Helpless" has to decide which will work best for her. She should explore a few questions such as when she feels stuck, what can she do to feel "un-stuck?" Is getting "un-stuck" an action or a mindset for her? Does she have to act her way out or think her way out of feeling stuck? For starters, she should stop lying to herself about what she cannot do and admit that she feels stuck because she is afraid. She has to admit that she is afraid of making the wrong choice and therefore she feels stuck.

Instead of making a list of reasons and circumstances that render her stuck, "The Helpless" should make a list of reasons she is choosing to stay. This will enhance her sense of control and therefore relieve her from feeling stuck. If she admits she is making a choice to stay with her cheating man rather than having no control over her inability to leave, she will drain the life out of her feeling of helplessness. Once she feels empowered from her sense of choice, she can then chart her path. Owning her choice will enable her to create a plan, complete with time frames and strategies that will render her un-stuck.

The Truth is, choosing to stay stuck in a rut is more about how she thinks and what she believes than what her man has done. Telling the truth means she will have to face the fears she has about leaving. The fears that have kept her stuck with him are the same fears that have kept her stuck in every other situation or circumstance in her life. She will also need to challenge her methodical way of thinking and the equational patterns of reasoning. To get unstuck, she will have to abandon the systematic approach to life that has kept her in unfavorable circumstances. This is what limits her choices and leaves her feeling stuck. "The Helpless" needs to get out of her head to get out of her own way, but until then she will continue to feel stuck.

# I DON'T WANT TO START OVER

A relationship is an investment. It is an investment of time and energy towards a goal of obtaining the heart's desires. When deciding to invest in a relationship, women often start with the end in mind. As soon as the first date, women evaluate and assess whether they have a potential *keeper*. We filter everything through the potential for a long-term relationship. The assessment starts at the end of the first date.

The evaluation and assessment continue after the first date with the woman carefully scrutinizing her date's character traits regarding what she is seeking in a man. She measures his earning potential and credit against the financial security she seeks. She screens his lifestyle and values to determine if he is a man with whom she envisions enjoying spending time. Is he kind, respectful, considerate, and affectionate? Does he relate well to her friends and family, and does he have a pleasant sense of humor? She watches for signs of how well he controls his anger, and his ability to express his feelings appropriately. By the end of the first month, a character profile has been developed, and the woman has determined whether to continue to invest or pull out and cut her losses. Once she commits to the investment, she is in it for the long haul.

When the evaluation and assessment are completed, the woman enters the planning process. She charts out their future and is careful to put into the relationship what she wants to get back. Her time is his time, she focuses all energy on him; he is the main character in her life story. Her soul is linked to his. The slide show running in her mind depicts the fairytale life that she and her man will have together. She envisions a life of bliss including romantic outings, intimate conversations, shared interests, toe-curling sex, quality time, and lots of laughter. She is ready to invest her all to create the perfect life with him exactly as envisioned in her mind. The investment is sealed, and she is ready to make a long-term commitment.

Now, let's fast forward through the slide show to the devastating part where the fairytale becomes a nightmare. That horrible moment when she found out her man was cheating. Just as if she had pushed the rewind button on the slide show, her mind races back through the past for signs, symptoms, and warnings of trouble in their relationship. She cannot believe or understand why this is happening and wants to know how she missed it. Once the emotions have run their course, the rational side of her brain ignites. The investment is measured as she reflects on time, energy, and resources committed to the relationship. Time in days, weeks, months, and years is calculated. Energy and resources to build a solid life together, and to make her vision materialize, is recounted. She has invested too much to just walk away, but how does she stay with the amount of loss that she feels? Here is where "The Helpless" is born.

Helplessly, she combs through the details of what she thought they had, which was a mutually satisfying, exclusive, monogamous relationship. She takes inventory of everything she has invested in the relationship. Helplessly, she lists all she gave, sacrificed, and did to make the relationship work. The list looks a bit like this:

- I've been there since _____.
- I helped him get _____.
- I gave up _____ for him.
- I sacrificed my _____ for him.
- I stuck with him through _____.
- I was there when he needed _____.
- I never asked him for _____.
- I always put his needs before mine.

After taking inventory, "The Helpless" does what most would. She weighs the pros and cons of staying or leaving. Most women feel that this exercise will help to clarify the right decision, but it often magnifies the feeling of helplessness. Too much has been invested, and she would lose too much. Too many questions about the future are unanswered with too many risks to count. Just like watching hard-earned money that was invested in the stock market disappear in a poor economy, "The Helpless" sees her efforts to build a healthy relationship shattered.

If the stock market crashes, would you pull out the investment that is left or keep investing, hoping to recoup what it has lost? She thinks about the relationship in the same way. Should she pull away from her cheating man and take all that she has left, or should she stay and try to work with what she has? Just as the stock investments would have lost value, "The Helpless" feels the value of the relationship has dropped because of the cheating. The biggest risks in staying with him are, he may cheat again, and she may not recover from the betrayal.

With each time he cheated, and she stayed, her sense of helplessness intensifies. After the first affair, she was so broken that she could not imagine ever healing or ever being with him again. After she cried a million tears, put her heart on lockdown, and vowed never to be deceived again, she did the opposite. She healed, and she gave him another chance. Why? Because she had invested too much and did not want to start over with someone new. She felt she knew what she had in him, she was comfortable, and she loved him enough to give him a second chance.

Re-investing in the relationship meant keeping tabs, taking notes, and constantly calculating gains and losses. Sadly, she never realized how helpless she had become while trying to avoid being cheated on again. She never fathomed if she had to do all this tracking, it was proof that he had not changed. It was proof things were still suspect, and he was giving her reasons to turn into a private investigator. She realized the relationship was not the same.

As "The Helpless" fights to stay on top of what is going on in her relationship, she finds out her man has cheated again. Shattered, disillusioned, furious, and vulnerable, she starts an internal debate about whether it would be worse to start over with someone new or to stay with the cheater she knows. The thought of starting over with another man zaps her last ounce of energy, leaving her with nothing left to give. With nothing left to give, she helplessly stays and gives him nothing. She gives him no more quality time, no more affection, no more trust, no more soul-ties, no more energy attempting to avoid being cheated on again. "The Helpless" stays because it doesn't require her to give, but what she doesn't realize is she will never be happy in this emotionally void relationship.

She knows that he will cheat again, but she tells herself she does not care. Because she has moved her boundary lines away from what she felt was her property, she has created space and time for him to do exactly what he has done in the past. There are no requirements for him to meet that might increase the chances of him changing. Helplessly, she has locked herself in this relationship with her cheating man because she has decided she does not want to start over.

"The Helpless" feels that giving of herself in a new relationship is too risky. The costs outweigh the benefits as she ponders the inventory of how much time, energy, and love she has poured into this relationship. She did her best and gave her all; he cheated repeatedly. Several times, she has concluded it would be better to leave him and be single rather than to put up with his continuous cheating. Already feeling empty, she can only imagine how lonely it would be if she were single. Her biggest fears have been, if she leaves she would end up being alone and lonely, or with another cheater. For these reasons, she helplessly opts to stay with someone who she cannot trust, will not invest in, and cannot allow back into her heart.

Helplessly, she continues to go through the motions. The relationship won't grow because it's not being fed. Not wanting to start over with someone new, and staying with her cheater, has left her defeated. In any game, the moment the player feels defeated is the moment they start to lose. The lie that keeps her stuck is telling herself she has nothing to lose because she will not recommit to the relationship. The Truth is, every time he cheats or violates her boundaries, she is losing something.

"The Helpless" says she doesn't want to start over with someone new. Just as the new person will be a stranger, she doesn't realize she now feels like her man is a stranger. She thought she knew him, but now feels she doesn't know the man who lied and cheated. The love he professed is questionable. The Truth is, every time she gives her cheating man another chance, she is starting over again. She tells herself that she doesn't want to be subjected to the games people play while trying to get to know one another, but that is exactly what she is doing with him each time that she takes him back.

She says she doesn't want to start over, and that is a lie that she tells herself. What she means is, she doesn't want to risk hooking up with another cheater. Also, she doesn't want to be fooled or have her trust betrayed again by someone new. Each time her man has betrayed her trust, "The Helpless" has lost a bit more hope in the concept of a faithful man. Because of her choice to stay with *a cheater,* a faithful man has now become a mythical character. The Truth is, she wants to start over, however, she has lost all faith in the belief that she could leave him and meet someone who doesn't cheat. She keeps voluntarily starting over with her cheating man, who is the type of man she doesn't want to risk meeting if she ever left.

When "The Helpless" is ready to see the truth about the lie that she doesn't want to start over, she can then restructure her thoughts and get unstuck. The Truth is, each time her man has cheated, and she stayed, she started over with a new image of him that became more and more tarnished. She doesn't have a choice about whether she will start over. Starting over is an automatic occurrence. She will have to start over if she stays, if she meets someone new, and if she is alone. The lie she is telling herself is keeping her stuck in a lifeless, loveless relationship with a man she no longer trusts and no longer feels she knows. The Truth is, starting over is mandatory, but whom she starts over with is optional.

# HE KNOWS HOW MUCH HE HURT ME SO HE WON'T CHEAT AGAIN

No matter how you find out that your man has been cheating, the news is crippling. Whether you become a private investigator who follows leads to evidence or blindsided by the discovery, the news paralyzes most into a state of helplessness. The hurt is so bad that it shuts down your ability to think and function, like a computer crashing from a virus. Trying to find words descriptive enough to express to your man how what he is doing makes you feel becomes an emotional monologue. The hurt, pain, and betrayal felt because of his cheating give birth to "The Helpless."

After the crippling news of the affair, "The Helpless" struggles to mend the wounds and to find her way through the days, weeks, and months that follow. Her best defense is to put up both emotional and physical walls. The only communication she has with him is to reiterate how his selfish, lowdown, cheating ways destroyed her emotionally. It has become her life's mission to make him understand how deep his cheating cut. Once he convinces her that "he gets it," and he has digested the bitter pill she had to swallow, then she can move on. Until then, she is stuck with evoking insight within him that gives him the ability to empathize with her pain.

There is a problem with the approach of getting him to understand her pain. With this approach, she has to stay wounded and broken to heighten his awareness of her pain and suffering. How will she know when he understands how badly his cheating hurt? What will be the signs of his awakening? By now, he has probably apologized, maybe cried, and possibly begged for forgiveness. So, what would be the deciding factor of when he understands? How will he show he cares about her feelings? This is a tricky situation.

What normally results from attempting to make him understand her pain? He feels sorrow and pity for her because of her brokenness. Feeling sorry for and pitying her won't change him. She has remained in a fragile state long enough for him to understand how badly he wounded her, but there is no guarantee that this will stop his cheating. He may pacify her to increase her sense of security, but eventually, sorrow and pity turn into frustration. Her wounded emotional state will be more of a burden to him than a teacher.

Here's the truth; what they have shared is an emotional reaction to his cheating. Her consistent reminders of how deep her wounds are, and her melancholy demeanor may provoke guilt and shame. This is not, and should not be mistaken for, a heightened level of understanding of how badly he hurt her. He may accommodate some of her demands and be able to say the right things, but there is no guarantee her hurt will convert him from his cheating ways.

If knowing how severely a woman was hurt by a man's cheating had the power to stop him from ever cheating again, then there would be no *cheaters*. There would only be *men who have cheated*. This theory of knowledge having the power to transform behavior hasn't proven to be foolproof. Knowledge alone has never changed his inappropriate behavior, corrected his bad habits, or transformed his character flaws. If she thinks her man will stop cheating because he knows how much he has hurt her, she is lying to herself.

"The Helpless" stays with her man because she wants to believe that he is sincere about all the promises he made after being caught cheating. How many women have been betrayed by their men, taken them back, and had their hearts broken again? How many women end up finding out that their cheating men were no different after they had made promises to change? How long does she have to stay wounded for him to remain faithful? How long will it take her to heal if she remains consistently in a wounded state?

To cure herself from being "The Helpless," she needs to go back over their relationship history. She has to be honest in her assessment because the person who she will be lying to is herself. An accurate assessment of whether she is with a *cheater or a man who has cheated* is necessary. If she is with a *man who has cheated,* and his pain is caused by his inappropriate behavior, then she is probably on point with her belief that he most likely won't cheat again. However, if the assessment shows she is with a *cheater*, chances are, he will not be changed by how much she hurts. The hurt, regret, and shame that he feels are "in the moment," and he is prone to cheat again once the moment passes.

Her man wants her to stop hurting, but that does not mean he will stop cheating. A *cheater's* choices are always about him, although he will be first to blame his woman. His cheating has always been about getting his needs met and not about tending to her needs. He will keep doing what he does because he is who he is, and nothing outside of his own needs will cause him to change.

"The Helpless" is not your typical victim; there is a method to her madness. She believes that she knows her man's character, and overall, she sees him as a decent person. She believes that he normally does the right thing when given a chance; he has a big heart, and therefore, he will stop cheating once he knows how much she is hurting. What she overlooks are all the character flaws that make him a *cheater*. To be a *cheater,* he has to be selfish, comfortable lying, deceiving, and manipulating. To engage in repeated acts of infidelity, his conscience is misaligned with traditional morals and values of fidelity in committed relationships. His values are inconsistent with hers, and it has set his moral compass on self-gratification. He has a problem with self-discipline and his sense of entitlement, not his feelings for her, allows him to continue to cheat.

The Truth is, until she is ready to reassess his character, this lie will keep her stuck. Maybe her assessment was realistic once upon a time, but it doesn't appear to be accurate now. An accurate assessment will gather the information needed to develop a deeper understanding of the subject. Here is a list of questions that she should ask herself for clarity:

- How long has he been cheating and lying to her in the process?

- How many times has he tried to convince her that his lies were the truth?

- How much time has he spent plotting to enable him

to cheat?

- How often has he been with other women and neglected obligations and promises made?

- How many times has he seen her hurt in the past while he was cheating?

- How many times has he treated her poorly while cheating?

After truthfully answering these questions, she will be better able to judge what change is likely. She will be able to formulate a clearer picture of what to expect from the man she believes will stop cheating "because he knows how much he hurt her." If she is honest, she will have to admit that the decent character traits she thought would correct his cheating are buried beneath his habitual, self-gratifying ways. Maybe her assessment will conclude that he selectively uses his ability to judge right from wrong. She may have to admit that when it concerns cheating, he will choose to do what feels right to him and not what is right for her.

The Truth is, the longer he has been cheating, the more likely this behavior has become a lifestyle rather than a lapse in good judgment. This lifestyle includes habitual lying, scheming, and manipulating to conceal his cheating. The longer this has been his lifestyle, the harder it will be for him to change. The frequency of cheating will determine whether this has become a sustained lifestyle. Habitual patterns are harder to break than random acts of indiscretion. The longer her man has been hooking up to have sex with other women, the stronger his bond will be to the lifestyle. That bond will be stronger than his will to change. "The Helpless" will have to strengthen her bond with her values and morals to break this cycle. To get unstuck, she will have to accept The Truth; her cheating man is not about to change because of knowing how much he hurt her.

# MAYBE THIS IS GOD'S WILL FOR MY LIFE

Have you ever dealt with the same problem repeatedly? Have you gotten out of one bad relationship only to find the same problems are creeping up in the new relationship? Have you ever felt that you were being pranked, and cameras were hidden somewhere because you couldn't possibly be going through the same drama again? Well, if your answer is *yes* to any of the above questions, you have probably become a member of "The Helpless" club.

*"Why is this happening to me?", "What did I do to deserve this?", and "What is the lesson for me in all of this?"* are typical questions that play through "The Helpless" head amid her challenges. When every man she has dated, from the first boy she labeled her boyfriend, to the last man she called hers has cheated, it makes her scratch her head. She questions what it is about her that makes every man she has ever dated end up cheating? It makes her wonder what she's doing wrong, and what she doesn't have that makes men cheat? At this point, she hasn't joined "The Helpless" club, but if she answers these questions wrong, she is well on her way. Right now, she's thinking if she can figure out the answers she can fix herself and her man will be faithful.

Reconstruction begins the minute she questions her role in his infidelity. She changes everything about herself. She changes her hairstyle, maybe even the color. Her style of fashion is upgraded or downgraded, depending on what her man likes. Where she will go and what she will do changes according to his preferences. She doesn't even recognize herself because she has altered so many aspects of her core identity. Everything comes to a screeching halt when she finds out that her man is still cheating despite all of her efforts.

With no earthly answers for this continuous cycle, and nothing left to change about herself, she looks upward. *"God, give me direction; tell me what to do; lead me down the right path; block me from the wrong man and show me the way"* are all common petitions of "The Helpless." She's seeking God's guidance therefore she knows it's best to follow the biblical commandments. Yes, she has a moral obligation to forgive her man, so she forgives him and moves forward. She's confident, now that she has prayed and forgiven him, God will take care of the rest. She surrenders it all to God, and then she finds out her man has cheated again. This is when she really believes *maybe this is God's will.*

Who doesn't desire the best that life has to offer? We want a good job, the perfect partner, a happy family, good friends, and to fulfill God's will. Most believe this is their birthright until life's challenges lead to a different point of view. When the same problem seems to keep recurring no matter what she does, how good she is, or how hard she tries, the belief that this must be God's will materializes. How could she believe it is her God-given destiny to spend her life with a cheating man? Maybe after being cheated on repeatedly, this belief will numb the pain because it's easier to accept God's will for her life than walk away from a bad relationship. If she believes it is God's will for her to be with a cheater, then she will adapt to the mindset that she has to obey. This belief will cushion her from feeling flawed and rejected because, if it's God's will for her to be with a cheater, there is nothing wrong with her.

She becomes "The Helpless" because, if this is God's will for her life, then she doesn't have a choice in the matter. She has to stay, and she lies to herself about her ability to do so without feeling stupid, used, and weak. She expects that she will no longer agonize over whether he will cheat again, because if this is God's will, he definitely will cheat again. The Truth is, because she is wounded and vulnerable, she doesn't have the ego strength to leave. This belief makes it necessary for her to stay with a cheating man, and she prays for God's strength to endure. Helplessly, she settles for much less than she desires and deserves in a man. She rationalizes that this has to be God's will, otherwise she wouldn't keep hooking up with the same type of guy and reliving the same drama.

She should be ashamed of herself for blaming God for her choice of men. Believing the lie that this is God's will for her life is anesthesia. It dulls the pain of facing the truth. She will find no benefit in hiding from pain. Pain is a purifier and ends in healing. The Truth is, in her broken and rejected state, she continues to attract the wrong man because she never allows herself to heal. It is not God's will for her to live in a wounded and defeated state with a cheating man; this is her choice.

One thing I believe to be true is there is always a profit when we are in a situation that is God's will for our lives. If you are with *a man who has cheated* and not *a cheater,* there will be a profit if you decide to stay after the affair. *A man who has cheated* will feel remorse, hold himself accountable for his actions, and seek to not put himself in a position to cheat again. He will look within himself to seek wisdom to assist with making better decisions, and his woman will profit from his repentance. She will end up with a man who is ready to commit to a monogamous relationship. Staying with *a cheater* will render drastically different outcomes.

Staying with *a cheater* could make any woman feel this is her destiny. It is his nature to cheat therefore if she stays she will continue to be cheated on. Revisit the previous chapter entitled, *"All Men Are Cheaters."* There you will see the differences between *a cheater and a man who has cheated.* If "The Helpless" has repeatedly chosen to stay with *a cheater,* she cannot dismiss her decision as God's will. The life she is living is the one she has created. Maybe she needs to accept The Truth that this is her own will for her life.

If she wants to search her situation for God's will, she needs to shift her focus in a different direction. If being with her cheating man has enhanced her self-worth, her sense of wisdom, and her sense of purpose, she can say she is in pursuit of God's will for her life. If instead, she allows the cheater to diminish her self-worth, dull her sense of wisdom, and alter her sense of purpose, she is not striving for God's will. To get unstuck, she will have to allow the pain from the reality of her choices to engulf her in a way that builds character. She will have to seek wisdom amid the pain to magnify the truth rather than deny the truth. There is no wisdom to learn from living in a state of denial. Developing the courage to live in truth will be the beginning of living in God's will for her life.

Denial creates bondage and suffering because the truth always seeks exposure. If staying with *a cheater* makes her perpetually anxious, depressed, angry, bitter, or resentful, how does this honor God? How is she honoring God by staying with a man she knows isn't right for her out of fear? Does it honor God for her to be broken and defeated? By staying in the relationship with *a cheater*, she is in bondage rather than in God's will.

The Truth is, she confuses staying with her cheating man with forgiving him. The mere act of staying is not the same as forgiveness. If she simply stays without truly forgiving him, she will become helplessly bitter, helplessly resentful, and helplessly dissatisfied. These feelings will prevent her from ever having a healthy relationship with him. The longer she stays without forgiving, the more emotional damage she will suffer. There is no healing without forgiveness. She doesn't realize that it is possible to forgive and choose not to stay, and that leaving does not mean she hasn't forgiven.

If "The Helpless" wants to know God's will for her life, she should seek wisdom. If she wants wisdom, she should seek the truth. If she wants the truth, she should look at the facts. If she wants the facts, she should review the relationship history. If she wants to know in whose will she has been living, she should look at the end result. If her cheating man is the one who is reaping all the benefits of her staying, then The Truth is, she has actually been stuck living in his will and not God's.

# PART 6

# LIES

# "THE SETTLER"

# TELLS HERSELF

# AT LEAST I KNOW WHAT I HAVE WITH HIM

*"It could be worse; there are a lot of dogs out there; every couple has to deal with some drama; and "there are no perfect relationships,"* are some rationalizations "The Settler" has developed to justify her choice to stay with her cheating man. She knows beyond any shadow of a doubt her man is cheating, but she sees the glass as half-full rather than half-empty. Her man is cheating, but she believes it could be a lot worse with someone else. She is staying because she feels, *"At Least I Know What I Have With Him."*

The building blocks of this lie are the minimizing and bargaining that results in constantly settling for less than what she wants and desires. "The Settler" mentality develops when allowing recurrent, inappropriate behaviors and actions to play out in her relationship. She has convinced herself that she isn't accepting her man's cheating because after each affair she fusses, cusses, and sets new boundaries. He has been told repeatedly staying out all night is unacceptable, not answering his phone is unacceptable, lying about his whereabouts is unacceptable, and cheating is unacceptable. What she considers unacceptable is clear. However, each time she stays after an affair, her boundaries become watered down and are washed away. Staying after repeated violations of trust and respect is accepting his cheating, no matter how she dresses it up.

What exactly is she acknowledging about what she has with him? Is she professing to know that he will stay out late, not answer his phone when she calls, not be where he says he will be, and continue to cheat? Is she professing to know that he will continue to violate her boundaries, disregard her needs, and disrespect her as his woman? Yes, this is exactly what she is acknowledging, and by doing so she is invalidating her standards. His violation, disregard, and disrespect of her boundaries will continue, and she will settle for the opposite of what she designed them to prevent. She is dismissing her self-worth and settling for a cheater. She knows exactly what she has, but she is not acknowledging the truth.

"The Settler" will create a logical explanation to justify the decision to stay. The outer layers of her man's unacceptable, inappropriate behaviors will be peeled back to search for the things he is doing right. A pros and cons list will follow, and she will have to work extra hard to see pros amid a magnitude of cons. If you repeatedly sit down with pen and paper, drawing a line down the middle to convince yourself that there is good lurking in the multitude of boundary violations, beware that you are morphing into "The Settler."

The pros and cons list exercise has a way of being tricky and has set many women up to stay in unfavorable situations. What happens is the focus goes to the number of acts, events, and character traits instead of the magnitude of the offense. If she is able to list 5 unfavorable acts, events, or character traits compared to 15 good, mistakenly the rationale is that the good outweighs the bad. The error here is the weight, which should be her guide, not the quantity of offenses. If cheating is a heavy offense because trust is at the top of her list of needs, then even if it is 1of 5 entries on the list of cons compared to the 15 pros, the pros shouldn't outweigh the cons. She shouldn't allow cheating on the cons list to be overshadowed by her man giving her gifts, being a hard worker, and having a pleasant sense of humor on the pros list. If the pros and cons aren't measured according to the weight and magnitude of the offense, "The Settler" will end up lying to herself about the quality of the man.

The Truth is, she should strive to know herself better than she knows him. She should know what she has in herself and know her non-negotiable offenses. The lists of pros and cons should be based primarily on her needs and values. At the end of the day, she should be proud of what she accepts on both lists. Here is an accurate interpretation of her lists when the cons are fewer but carry more weight than the pros, and she stays:

- I know that my man is a cheater, and if I stay, I have to deal with that.

- I will accept the good things that he does as re-payment for the cheating.

## At Least I Know What I Have With Him

- I will allow him to lie to me, and I will lie to myself about how I feel about staying with a cheater.

- I will forgive him for cheating again as long as I can list some pros.

- I will accept his measure of my worth to stay with him.

The only cure for "The Settler" mentality is, "To Thine Own Self Be True." This is not a selfish way of thinking or acting, it is about self-care. While her man is looking out for his needs, she should look out for hers. She needs to be honest with herself about what she can and cannot accept in a partner and her life. She has to stop lying to herself, acting as if she can accept the unacceptable. Her non-negotiable offenses shouldn't be devalued, and the weight shouldn't be minimized.

If his actions, behaviors, and traits take away from her self-worth, impair her self-image, and stifle her self-expression, she is truly settling for self-sabotage. She will feel insecure, bitter, resentful, and depressed because she is violating her value system to stay with a cheating man. What will probably happen is over time she will have to disconnect from herself to stay with him. "The Settler" will never have peace in this relationship because she has to disregard herself to stay. She knows that she deserves better, but she is settling for less because her list of pros and cons makes her believe that the good outweighs the bad.

Let's have her flip the script and say, "At least I know who I have to be to stay with him." This way of processing it puts a totally different spin on things and clarifies her image of who she has become. She will gain clarity about what her future will look like with him. If she flips the script and analyzes who she has to become, she can decide between leaving or staying before the damage to her self-worth, self-image, and self-expression is irreversible. The list of pros and cons should comprise how much she will have to settle for if she stays.

The Truth is, "The Settler" is lying to herself about staying with her man because she knows what she has with him.

## The Truth About The Lies

Who stays with a man whom they know will continue to cheat and can truthfully respect their decision? Who stays with a man whom they know will continue to cheat and will feel securely anchored in the relationship? Who stays with a man whom they know will continue to cheat and honestly feels confident that his actions will honor her existence as his woman? This lie will cause her to become emotionally numb by default and cause her to be less reactive to his cheating. The emotional walls she feels are creating a protective barrier for her feelings will create an emotional box for her to live inside. She won't be able to put the walls down because she continuously has to protect her heart from the pain of his cheating. There will be no way for genuine love to develop in this relationship, and what will exist is an unhealthy attachment to one another.

If she cannot respect her decision to stay with him, she will continuously feel disrespect. The inability to feel securely anchored in their relationship will always cause her to feel vulnerable. She will inevitably feel disconnected from him and herself if she does not feel her man's actions honor her as his woman. If she continuously feels disrespected, always feels vulnerable and inevitably disconnected, she will undoubtedly lose herself, piece-by-piece, the longer she stays.

What she is missing is The Truth; the walls she has created as a protective barrier from hurt are creating a barrier to honoring her values, needs, and desires. She can choose to stay behind the walls of lies and keep her man "as is," or she can tear down the walls and honor her boundaries, needs, and desires. The Truth is, if "The Settler" recovers and reconnects the pieces she lost while trying to stay with her cheating man, she can change the way she makes decisions. Her decisions will reflect respect for her values, become securely anchored in getting her needs met, and confidently accepting into her life only that which honors her truth. Knowing what she has with him will no longer be a positive selling point for staying stuck with her cheating man.

# BEING WITH MY CHEATING MAN IS BETTER THAN BEING ALONE

As early as childhood, women are conditioned for committed relationships. Just watch any little girl play with her dolls. Normally, she will mimic the role of the mother. Now, if there is a little boy around, she will try to convince him to put down his action figures and play "house." If you continue to watch, you will see the little girl coach the little boy through the motions of how to play the role of the father and her partner. In reality, this scenario continues to play out throughout life with the woman coaching the man on how to be the partner she wants, needs, and desires.

Because girls have been role-playing this relationship stuff throughout life, it makes sense that some women are not comfortable being alone. We live in a society tailor-made for couples. How often do you see a table for one in a restaurant? The only single seat on a bus is the bus driver's seat. There are even numbers of seats in each row at the movie theater that implies the expectation of people coming in pairs and groups. We are conditioned to expect to be with someone throughout life, therefore being alone is often avoided with a high price. If not careful, this mentality will give way to the birth of "The Settler."

"The Settler" mentality is not natural; it is born out of fear. When the little girl plays "house" she depicts the perfect home life, complete with everything she desires. When the teenager thinks about dating, she envisions a Prince who will love her unconditionally, cherish her existence, and cater to her emotional need. Throughout the teen and young adult years, following a series of substandard relationships resulting in heartbreak, disillusionment takes over the fairytale. The belief in the *"happily ever after"* dismantles, and the *"take what you can get"* mentality takes root. By the time the girl becomes a woman, some are firmly rooted in "The Settler" mentality out of the fear of being alone.

    I do not know many women who are happy to confess that they believe being with a cheating man is better than being alone. No woman is excited about, or able to maintain her self-respect by doing so. Being alone is not a goal that many women strive for or welcome with open arms. Sure, she has tried being alone after failed relationships, but everybody keeps trying to set her up as if there is something wrong with being single. The single woman reassures her friends and family that she is happy by herself, but then she ventures out into a world that caters to couples. Eventually, being single feels lonely, sad, wrong, and pitiful. The longer she is single, the more she fears growing old alone, not having someone to share her life with, and ending up a lonely old lady. These experiences lead to the formation of "The Settler" mentality.

    If the belief that *being with a cheating man is better than being alone* is what keeps her locked in the relationship, then maybe she has never advanced from being the little girl in the make-believe world with the little boy. She could create a fantasy by role-playing back then, and maybe she still has that ability. She has to be extremely creative to convince herself there is value in being with a cheater. Her role hasn't changed because she is still trying to coach him on how to be the partner she wants, needs, and desires. However, his role has changed quite a bit because he is not the compliant, conforming, and accommodating playmate she had as a girl. Nonetheless, she has created a fantasy world where it is better to be with him than to be alone.

    Maybe "The Settler" needs to rev up her creative juices and develop *The Middle*. She has been operating from a point of tunnel vision where she has lied to herself to believe it is better to be with her cheating man than to be alone. This lie has serious blind spots where she refuses to see things "as is." *The Middle* is derived from a timeline of the actual relationship. All the details of his affairs, how she felt, how he treated her, and what she sacrificed to stay should be included. *The Middle* is the place of truth, where her feelings are buried alive, never to be considered again. Developing *The Middle* will force her to test the reality of how it has been to be with him. She will now have to use the facts versus the fantasy to make a realistic assessment about whether being with a cheating man is better than being alone.

Creating a timeline of the relationship will lead her to look at the facts and release the lies. If she went back down memory lane, in six-month to one-year intervals, and filled in *The Middle* of each time frame with how she felt about the affairs, how he treated her, and what she has gained and loss, she could then re-evaluate the belief that being with a cheating man is better than being alone. A timeline that lists the facts by eliminating minimizations, rationalizations, and generalizations could assess the actual value in staying with him over being alone. Releasing how they are perceived as a couple and envisioning how she can thrive as a single woman could assist with challenging this belief. Her timeline could assist with seeing that in reality, being with a cheating man has caused her to feel alone; it has created a lonely existence. It could lead her to believe being single is not so bad after all.

It is very important that she knows who she is and acknowledges her core values. The ability to live in truth and accept the fact that your man is cheating, while not feeling devalued, is "do-able" for some women. "The Settler" has to be truthful about whether she is one of those women. If she doesn't need fidelity and doesn't feel insecure because of her man's cheating, then being with her cheating man is better than being alone. If she doesn't become depressed, anxious, or consumed with his cheating, then being with him is better than being alone. Finally, if a man cheating is not on her "non-negotiable list," not a violation of her value system, and doesn't forced her to accept what she finds morally unacceptable, then being with her cheating man is better than being alone.

The Truth is, if she is not one of those women who can deal with her man cheating and she considers cheating a major deal-breaker, then being with him is not better than being alone; she is *settling*. If being with a cheating man makes her crazy, paranoid, or clingy, and she still stays, then being with him is not better than being alone; she is *settling*. The Truth is, "The Settler" does not really believe it is better to be with a cheating man; she is just staying with him because she is afraid to be alone. She has created an anxious fantasy about her future and being alone, which makes her cling to what she has. If she would take the time to create *The Middle* and differentiate between being alone and being single, she may be able to create the life that she wants and deserves. This is the only way she can create a life that complements her rather than keeps her stuck with a cheating man. The Truth is, being with her cheating man is not better than being alone, but it is lonely.

## I DON'T CARE ANYMORE
## SO HIS CHEATING CAN'T HURT ME

After she has stayed with her cheating man, hoping he would clean up his act and show her who he really is, "The Settler" resorts to the defense mechanism of not caring. She attempts to brainwash herself into believing she doesn't care that he continues to cheat. This nonchalant attitude allows her to remain in the relationship without admitting that she is settling for behavior she vowed never to accept. *"I don't care"* is an emotional wall, erected around her heart, so she won't have to feel the pain of living a lie. Of course, she cares about his cheating, and without a doubt, it hurts.

*"I don't care"* is the emotional equivalent to anesthesia for a painful wound. It dulls the pain but doesn't heal the wound. Just as anesthesia numbs the pain, the *"I don't care"* attitude numbs the emotions. This numbness creates a safe barrier and blocks her connection to her cheating man on an emotional level. "The Settler" becomes mechanical, practical, and methodical in her dealings with him. I wonder what would happen if she dared to admit, she cares?

Of course, her preference is to feel secure in her relationship. Nobody wants to live behind walls, but sometimes comfort can be found in discomfort. False security can exist in the familiarity of discomfort, but trust and mutual respect will never exist in discomfort. Ironically, she finds a false sense of security in knowing her man will cheat again, not in expecting him to change. Unfortunately, finding security in the familiar, uncomfortable situation will lead to a long-term relationship with misery.

Because she tells herself that she doesn't care, she can now remove herself from the emotional hook of being rattled by her man's cheating. She will no longer have such a powerful reaction to his lies. In essence, she is trying to simplify her life by settling for the flawed relationship rather than continuously experiencing disappointment felt by the expectation of change. She definitely will not set herself up for failure in a new relationship. If she knew what the future held the first time her man cheated and she stayed, she would have cut her losses and ended the relationship. Now that she has bound herself to a repeat offender, her only recourse is "to not care." This is the lie she created to shield her heart from further hurt.

Deciding not to care about her man cheating reflects a spiritual and emotional death. She has a defeated spirit and disabled emotions. The outcome is the death of her dreams, her happiness, and her ability to trust. Also, there is the death of hope and longing for anything better. She is the walking dead in this relationship, survived in death by her cheating man.

"The Settler" does not realize what she is allowing to happen while accepting his cheating. She thinks she is smart, but it is never smart to lie to yourself. She tells herself that if her man is going to cheat anyway, why not just expect the inevitable? She labels herself a realist who can accept the truth. In reality, she is in denial because she does care that her man continues to cheat, and it hurts. Because denial camouflages the hurt, bitterness, and resentment, she becomes cynical about love. She will not dare seek a healthy relationship with a new man. Choosing to stay with her cheating man has altered her entire belief system regarding intimate relationships. Because she does not want to admit her error in staying after he cheated the first time, she now has to lie to herself about not caring and being immune to future hurt.

If we analyze why she created the lie, we will discover that lying is easier than admitting she wasted her time, energy, and tears on a man who will never be who she needs him to become. "The Settler" is protecting her choices and emotions by staying. She believes leaving will cost more than staying because she lies to herself about the price of staying. The Truth is, staying has caused her to become bitter, and she cringes whenever she hears a love story. Whenever someone speaks about how wonderful their man is, and how much love they share, she is quick to shock them into reality. She will not hesitate to cast the shadow of doubt on the authenticity of their commitment. Staying has caused resentment that has disabled her ability to expect and receive love.

Bitterness and resentment have limited her access to the truth and keep her chained to a lie. *"I don't care"* grew out of bitterness and has limited her access to love, resulting in her unwillingness to give and receive love. The Truth is, she has always and will always want genuine love, but she fell out of love with her cheating man following the first affair. She settled because she did not know any better. The truth will allow her to know better and expect better. The Truth is, the love she has been withholding from her cheating man is the love she is withholding from herself. Maybe he can't hurt her anymore, but she will continue to hurt herself if she doesn't allow herself to care.

"The Settler" has put up a good fight to avoid living in truth and does not realize that "truth" can be her saving grace. If she allows the truth to surface, the pain she fears will work in her favor. It would reignite her ability to feel and express her emotions, causing the emotional walls she built, to protect her from hurt, to fall down. She would understand the walls were creating a coffin, not a protective shield. If she allows herself to feel the pain and starts healing from the betrayal and disregard, her tears would eventually give way to clear vision. She will see herself, her partner, and her predicament exactly "as is." Denial will no longer be her constant companion, and truth will release her from the bitterness and resentment.

When she is ready to stop lying about not caring if he cheats, she will acknowledge betraying herself, face her regrets, and rebuild her ability to process the truth. By accepting her reality, she can reclaim her core beliefs and values. Only then will she regain her ability to love herself and others and cease to accept the lies she created as an emotional shield. When she accepts the truth, her lies will feel like an insulting waste of time. Willingness to tell herself the truth will empower her to care.

The Truth is, she will have to accept the fact that the person who is cheating on her is "her." She stopped caring about her feelings, needs, values, and security. Instead, she lied by creating the belief that she doesn't care about her man cheating. She will have to admit that while she was blaming him for all the hurt, pain, and betrayal she felt, the bulk of the damage was self-inflicted. "The Settler" will have to accept the truth that she has stayed with a cheater because it bothers her too much to face the reality of wasted time, energy, and tears. She made the mistake of repeatedly staying, believing he would change, and exhausted her energy by hoping and looking for a change that was not there. Facing the truth will hurt, but it is the only way for her to get unstuck and create the life she wants and deserves.

# PART 7

# LIES

# "THE SAVIOR"

## TELLS HERSELF

# I WANT TO SAVE MY RELATIONSHIP

Most would agree, women are the traditional caretakers and nurturers. They live life sacrificially for the greater good of those they love. If the long-term effect of her caretaking, nurturing, and sacrificing is positive, then she thrives. However, when her hard work and efforts don't pay off, she easily becomes a martyr to die to self for the sake of others. This is no different in the relationship with her cheating man. She will do whatever it takes to save their relationship because she believes in the power of sacrifice. Unbalanced sacrificing leads to the making of "The Settler."

Research studies have theorized that women more often than men are feelers. This possibly enhances their ability to expect existing unfavorable circumstances to result in positive outcomes. When rescuing a failing relationship, the woman is typically the one to put the "S" on her chest and become "The Savior." Maybe more instinctively than men, women aim to create secure, loving, mutually exclusive relationships. Women also see the potential for "forever" even when a relationship is showing signs of distress. These are reasons a woman would be more prone to morph into "The Savior," taking on the impossible mission of rescuing the relationship.

What exactly does the word *save* mean when the woman says; *"I want to save my relationship"*? What exactly will saving the relationship require of her? Common synonyms for the word *save* are rescue, salvage, and revive. A savior is heroic, one who comes to make everything right, maybe even perform a few miracles along the way. It is possible but less common to hear about a rescue, salvage, or revival being accomplished single-handedly. Hence, doing this work in a failing relationship will more than likely require the efforts of them both. If her man is unmotivated and inactive with the mission to save the relationship, it will require her to work extra hard and maybe even perform a miracle.

Her goal of saving the relationship is a setup for failure if her motivation is not clear. She needs to start with a clear definition of the relationship and the problems. I guarantee she will struggle with assessing the relationship without filters that minimize the problems. She will probably set out to save the "potential" rather than what she has. If she is honest about what she has, she might have a fighting chance for success. Honestly assessing the man and the problems will allow her to know "when to hold them and when to fold them."

Before embarking on a mission to save the relationship, she should clarify a few questions. She should ask herself if the true mission to save the relationship is because of fear of being alone? Is her effort to save the relationship motivated by trying to avoid failure or feeling like a failure? She should ask if she is trying to avoid the opinions and ridicule of others if the relationship ends? Is she attempting to save the relationship because that's what the women in her family traditionally do? Last, she should be clear about whether she is trying to save the relationship primarily to avoid the pain that will follow a breakup?

If the answer to any of the questions above is *yes,* "The Savior" is wasting her time. The only relationship she can save is the one with herself. Learning to set relationship boundaries that assist with self-love is the key. She professes to love her cheating man so much that she wants to save the relationship. In reality, unless she has learned and practiced self-love, she cannot possibly love him. The Truth is, without self-love, all she has with him is an unhealthy attachment created by insecurity or desire for control. Without self-love, she cannot set the necessary boundaries that will lead to him treating her with respect and higher regard. Saving herself has to come before saving their relationship, and this requires honesty and clarity about her true motivation.

She needs to save the relationship because she has lost herself in her man. Somewhere along the way, she likely began sacrificing her values, desires, dreams, and goals to keep him. Keeping him and saving the relationship required repeatedly sacrificing and settling. "The Savior" has altered herself so much over the years she is now a shell of who she was when she met him. Undoubtedly, she has sacrificed and given too much to let the relationship end. Is it possible that she is attempting to save her investment in the relationship and not the relationship itself?

Some *saviors* will develop a passive role, and others

will become controlling to block their men from cheating. Some will walk on eggshells to avoid conflict or offending their men because they don't want to "make" him cheat again. Even if it means becoming numb to his cheating or losing herself, both will do whatever it takes to save the relationship. She has invested and sacrificed too much to let the relationship end.

All too often "The Savior" arrives at my office feeling broken. She speaks of how much she has *"put up with"* and *"given up"* to be with her cheating man. Her mood is either depressed or anxious, and there is a sense of restlessness in her spirit. The goal is to make the relationship right by making him embrace the changes she feels are necessary for a healthy relationship. Her man is cheating, and she is the one trying to identify changes he needs to make to save the relationship. She has tunnel vision and cannot see that this makes absolutely no sense.

What exactly has her relationship with herself become since she has repeatedly stayed with her cheating man? How much has she changed, departed from core values, and altered her belief system to save her relationship? What is her self-respect level, and how is it demonstrated? If she evaluated the problems in the relationship by utilizing her true value system, and not the one she has conformed to, would she continue to believe that the relationship is worth saving? She is lying to herself about wanting to save the relationship, because the relationship "as is" is not desirable?

The Truth is, "The Savior" never really stopped to ask what she is actually trying to save. She hasn't taken the time to assess what she would release if she were to embrace the truth. There has not been an honest evaluation of what saving the relationship would cost her and cause her to feel about herself. Maybe if she took the time to assess the answers to the questions above, she wouldn't be stuck lying to herself and single-handedly trying to save the relationship. Her assessment would end with the realization that the end of a relationship is not always a failure. She would know the only relationship she needs to save is the one with herself.

She truly does not want the relationship she has with her cheating man. Therefore, she is lying to herself about wanting to save their relationship. What she wants is for the relationship to change into one she desires. That would be a relationship with a faithful man, who shares her core values, so she doesn't have to continue deviating from her genuine needs. She desires a relationship that will allow her to be true to herself. "The Savior" desires a relationship, one that will foster self-respect and security. If she had this type of relationship, it would be worth saving. The Truth is, she doesn't want to save *this* relationship, but she has invested so much into it that she will continue to stay stuck with her cheating man because of the lie she tells herself.

# I'M A CHRISTIAN SO
# I HAVE TO FORGIVE HIM

"The Savior" lives by mandatory moral codes to forgive. The Bible says, *"Forgive those who trespass against you; forgive your enemies; forgive and you shall be forgiven."* Therefore, when she finds out her man has cheated, even though she feels disgusted by the sight of him, she believes that she has to forgive. Although she possesses the *savior mentality*, she is still human. Therefore, after going ballistic, losing her religion, and cursing the day she met him, she vows to forgive and expects what he has broken to be restored.

She typically miscalculates two outcomes. She believes that if she forgives, then God will bless her with a repentant and reformed man who will no longer cheat. She also believes that staying with him is a demonstration of forgiveness. Her misconception is thinking that *staying* and *forgiveness* are the same. Although she has committed to staying with him and has vowed to forgive, working through the hurt and betrayal will be a long journey.

I know this mistake in judgment is not limited to "The Savior." There are plenty of women who have fallen prey to the belief that staying is a condition of forgiving. Let's be clear, staying is not forgiving, and forgiving doesn't mean you have to stay. To stay thinking that it equates to forgiveness leads to bitterness and resentment. Forgiveness means you release the guilty cheater from his debt to you. He owes you nothing, and through grace and mercy, you release him from the debt of the betrayal. If "The Savior" does not do this, staying with him means nothing, and she has not truly forgiven.

The savior mentality does not make her a saint. There is still the spirit of vengeance underneath her halo. She vows to forgive, but she believes that God needs her help to reform her cheating man. She will stop at nothing to shame him into experiencing the hurt and pain that his cheating has inflicted upon her. She will beat him down with scriptures that magnify his sinful nature to ensure he will not cheat again. She will drag him to every ministry that deals with fornication, backsliders, and whore mongrels. Her true intent is to reform her cheating man, for God's sake.

Typically, her method of saving is an attempt to control his urge to cheat by becoming preachy and moralistic. Her goal is to create a sacred environment where cheating is not a possibility. She has not accepted the cheater back into her life to allow him to continue to cheat, so her goal is to spiritually transform him into the model partner she desires. She creates a relationship of bondage, hoping to develop a mutual agreement that cheating is unacceptable. Just as staying does not mean forgiving, bondage does not mean bonding. "The Savior" is sentencing her cheating man to live in her prison, in the name of forgiveness, to save the relationship.

True forgiveness will lead to freedom from bondage, vengeance, and control. Christian forgiveness will allow her to see her cheating man for exactly who he is without judgment. She would be able to accept that the man she has chosen has cheated, and his choice has nothing to do with her. The choice to cheat is just like the choice to forgive. It truly has little to do with the other person and everything to do with *you*. "The Savior" has no clue what true forgiveness is because she is too busy trying to *act like* a Christian.

Doesn't she realize that forgiveness is a principle of release and not a behavioral contract? She thinks it is her duty, as a Christian, to shine a light on all his transgressions, to re-order his steps. Her halo gives her X-ray vision, and she can see straight through her man's mess. Every time he looks at another woman, "The Savior" reminds him of how she forgave him, and how he needs to change his cheating ways from here on out. The Truth is, she has not yet forgiven him, but she will allow him to stay in her life until he has earned her forgiveness. She believes she has to stay with him to save him from himself and in the process save their relationship.

The trouble with "The Savior" is she does not have the insight to realize what she is doing. She ignorantly believes if she is willing to forgive, then she will end up with the faithful man she has always wanted. She doesn't approach the situation with a realistic view of who her man is and what he can change at this point. There is a hidden agenda. What she is doing is bargaining with God, because she believes that if she forgives his cheating, then God will change him into the man she wants. She is bargaining for this blessing in exchange for her forgiveness. Is that what Christian forgiveness is all about?

The Truth is, she is hiding behind Christianity, and she already knows that her man will never be faithful. If she can convince herself and others that she is honoring God's will, then she thinks she can stay and not feel foolish. The fact that she continues to remind him of his transgressions and monitors his every step is proof that she cannot endure the cheating with Christian forgiveness. Even though she lies to herself and him by saying she forgives him, her actions show her heart. She needs him to act a certain way before she can truly forgive. Forgiveness does not mean she automatically has to stay with her cheating man. The Truth is, she probably won't be able to forgive him until she leaves.

Many *saviors* are unaware of the progressive nature of healing and forgiving, and believe forgiveness automatically results in an instant change. The Truth is, "The Savior" defeats her healing by masking hurt and pain behind Christianity. She mistakenly believes that if she has forgiven, then she will no longer hurt. Her thinking is that forgiveness means to let go and letting go means no more hurt. This is not how forgiveness works.

Healing of anything and everything is a process and progresses in accordance to the extent of the wound or injury. Unless there is a miracle, there will be no automatic healing. Therefore, her feelings of betrayal and resentment will not automatically change. Because "The Savior" attempts to be a *super-saint,* who can forgive instantaneously, it forces her to lie. She lies to herself and everyone else to make believe she is not consumed by anger, hurt, and resentment. She acts like there is no lingering pain, like a person who has stepped on a nail trying to continue to walk normally. The nail causes actual pain and damage like the cheating, so until healing occurs she will experience recurrent emotional distress. Any hope of truly being able to forgive her man depends on her ability to accept the truth, allow the healing, and adjust to the emotional roller coaster that will follow. If she cannot do this, she will become a martyr.

Normally, martyrs are killed or suffer tremendously for their commitment; they sacrifice themselves for *the cause.* As a martyr for the relationship, "The Savior" dies a spiritual death because there is neither a connection between her and her man nor her and true forgiveness. The Truth is, she suffers in silence because she mistakes suffering for forgiveness. She is with *a cheater*, not *a man who has cheated*, and he will cheat again. Because she is a Christian who confuses *staying* with *forgiving* and is not truly committed to forgiveness, she will stay in this hell with her cheating man. The Truth is, if she forgives him from a place of true forgiveness, and not her Christian duty, then she can get unstuck from the hell that she has created.

# I DON'T WANT TO BREAK UP MY FAMILY

Whether married, cohabitating, or living apart, once a child is born most women shift immediately from *couple* to *family* mentality. *The family* becomes the priority and many sacrifices will follow. Building a healthy family life is her primary goal and the core of her existence. There is nothing more important than family.

It doesn't matter whether she grew up with both parents or in a single-parent home, the desire for a healthy family life is universal. If raised by both parents, she probably has been conditioned to believe a two-parent home is best for her child. If she grew up in a single-parent home, she might have longed to live in a two-parent home, and therefore strives to give her child what she didn't have. *Family* is important, and she will strive to save hers at all costs. This mindset becomes the glue that gels "The Savior" in the position to endure a world of pain and suffering.

To "The Savior," family needs trump individual needs most of the time. Doing all, sacrificing all, and being all for the family can create a lack of balance, and she will eventually lose sight of her individual boundaries. It will no longer matter how many times her man has fallen short and missed the mark because they are now family. She will fight to keep her family together. That's why she has stayed time and time again after he has cheated. She refuses to allow him or anyone to break up her family.

There is no doubt "The Savior" began screening her man for "long-term relationship potential" as soon as they met. Sure, there were a few pet peeves and a couple of red flags in the beginning. Maybe she told him what he needed to work on and he said he would. Perhaps, in the beginning, he sent his "representative," the wonderful person who made all the right promises and did all the right things. He could bamboozle her, and his authentic character didn't emerge until later in the courtship. She ignored her intuition. Time passed; she continued to date him and ended up pregnant; now they are a *family*. No matter what, "The Savior" will not break up her family.

What exactly is she trying to save? It's her prayer that anchors her, and she believes that someday she will have the perfect family life. She dreams that her man will be a positive and active part of her child's life, and they will enjoy quality time doing everything together. In her dream, they will share family values, agree on parenting issues, and have great communication. If her dream were to come true, they would have the ideal family and would be the envy of everyone they know. She is holding out for her dream to come true, which is why she vows she will not break up her family.

Before her man cheated the first time, she had their life together all mapped out. She envisioned they would be so in love. They would start family traditions and celebrations would be plentiful. With ease, they would share responsibilities, agree on finances, and have common interests. They would equally commit to fidelity and share a healthy, fulfilling sex life. It disrupted her vision when she realized he was not following the same script, and he was cheating. The script would have to be edited.

The realization of his cheating was earth shattering, and her dream became a nightmare. It ruined everything she had envisioned. Disillusioned and devastated, she focused on *"the family"* instead of *"the couple."* She convinced herself that she could still save *"the family"* even if his cheating meant they wouldn't be the ideal couple. "The Savior" put her desire for a healthy relationship with a faithful partner on the shelf next to the script she was following, and she vowed to save the family.

Before she put her dream-life script on the shelf, she assessed how the cheating could have happened. She thought she knew him and what he considered important. She believed that like her, he would always choose to do what was right for the family. It never dawned on her he would betray her and threaten the security of their family. She didn't think he was perfect, but she never envisioned him risking losing his family over another woman. After being caught off-guard, she had to choose whether to stay with her cheating man or break up the family. This was not a part of her script.

He begged and pleaded for another chance and vowed

never to cheat on her again. Because the threat of losing her made him realize how important she was, he said he couldn't imagine life without his family. This was what "The Savior" was longing to hear. Even though bruised, she was vulnerable to his promises. She wanted her family to stay intact, she wanted to believe him, and she wanted to have her dream become reality. How could she live with herself if she didn't give her family another chance? She couldn't, so she accepted his promises because she didn't want to break up her family.

Even though she had no idea how she would trust him again, she stayed. She felt like a fool for staying because she never imagined being a woman who would stay with a cheating man. Nonetheless, she believed it had to be done for the sake of the family. Now things would have to change because it was no longer about *"her,"* it was about *"the family."* When she committed to saving the family, she sacrificed her own needs and wants.

"The Savior" had to find a way to live with something she vowed never to accept. Despite her desire to leave and never look back, she stayed. She did what she had to do to make it work. Maybe they slept in separate rooms and she cut him off sexually. She could demand the usual stuff like changing the cell phone number, access to all of his social media, freedom to check his phone at will, and anything else that she could think of that made her feel a measure of control. She was doing what she needed to do to feed the lie that she was keeping the family together.

She was prayerful that he was speaking from the heart when he made all of those wonderful promises. Hopefully, he was being honest when he told her how much she meant to him and he couldn't imagine life without his family. If he meant what he said, then it would be worth every second she suffered because they would work together to save the family. He would be ready to be the family man in her script. "The Savior" would be making the right decision to stay if he was ready to change, because she wouldn't have to lie to herself anymore.

I don't doubt that she truly wanted to save her family, but could there have been other motives for staying with him? Could it be that she didn't want to be alone, raise a child alone, or be a statistic? Is it possible that her gut told her to leave him long before she got pregnant and gave birth, and because she didn't listen, she now feels guilty about leaving? Maybe she lied to herself and doesn't want to face the fact that they were never a family. Her image of what could be is what kept her stuck in the lie. The Truth is, her image of her family was always much stronger than the reality she was living.

"The Savior" will not take responsibility for her man's cheating, but she takes responsibility for not breaking up the family. She is overly concerned with what a breakup would do to her child. It would be unfair for the child to suffer because of the dad's stupidity. She could not stomach the guilt of the child crying because she left "daddy," and blaming her for breaking up the family. Her grandmother, mother, aunts, and cousins all stayed after their men cheated, so what gives her the right to leave? This is the guilt trip keeping her stuck with her cheating man.

She is lying to herself if she truly believes her choice to leave him would cause the family to break up. The Truth is, her man broke up the family when he chose another woman. He betrayed his family the second he contemplated cheating. He broke up the family with all the hours, days, weeks, and months that followed when he repeatedly cheated. He broke up the family and "The Savior" thinks it is her job to keep together what he tore apart.

Some couples have built a solid enough foundation that can survive infidelity. They have put in the work, and therefore able to re-establish trust after betrayal. Some couples become stronger and more connected after an affair because of their foundation. They commit to affair-proofing their relationship in the aftermath of the cheating. There are women who can truly forgive their men for cheating and not be haunted by the affair for life. "The Savior" has to commit to being honest about what she has and who she is.

Trying to save her relationship through what she does for her family will never work. She will never feel fulfilled by just being "The Savior" for the family. There will always be a void, and a sense of emptiness, if all of her efforts are for her family. Staying with him will have to be for *"her"* and benefit *"her"* for her family to feel authentic. If all she accomplishes is keeping the label *"family"* intact, it will be impossible for her and her cheating man to have a healthy bond. What will result is her feeling used, taken for granted, and disrespected. A strained relationship with him will develop, and she will be continuously *giving, doing,* and *being* without receiving.

Trying to save children by keeping the family together rarely works in their best interest when the mother and father do not have a healthy relationship. Unless the children are in a home, where they witness warmth and compassion, trust and honesty, and sharing and caring, it is more of a disservice to them for the parents to stay together. If they are not witnessing healthy communication patterns, effective conflict resolution, and mutual respect, "The Savior" is lying when she tells herself staying is saving the family. Staying is actually aiding the breakup. If staying with her cheating man fragments her, then the family will be broken. Staying under these conditions will never benefit the children.

The Truth is, re-thinking her traditional concept of "the family" is necessary. The mommy and daddy don't have to live under the same roof, or be a couple, to be a family. She will have to accept that whether she and her cheating man stay together, they and their child will always be family. If she will abandon traditional thinking, she can create a peaceful family life for her child. Once she tells the truth about what she has and what she needs, she can piece the fragments of her life back together. Until then, The Truth is, staying is contributing to her being broken and stuck with a cheating man.

# I HAVE TO GIVE HIM A CHANCE TO CHANGE

Let's set the record straight. "The Savior" is not a weak woman who can't maintain personal boundaries. Her actions may cause some men to experience her as naïve, but naïve she is not. She is a woman of principle, abiding by traditional morals and values. Her beliefs lead her along the path of forgiveness and second chances. Conflict arises when she repeatedly has to abandon her own needs to give someone else a chance to show change.

The path to "a chance to change" is long and bumpy. Her man cheated, she found out, and the relationship is pretty much over. She tells herself she can never trust him again and believes a relationship without trust is impossible. Trust is the building block and the cornerstone of true emotional intimacy for most women, and "The Savior" is no different. If you asked her to list five things considered most important for a successful relationship, she would place trust at the top of her list. That is why the first time her man cheated, she was done. At least that is what she told herself. Because we are talking about giving him a chance to change, we know there was a change of heart.

We've all heard the saying, "Time heals all wounds." I'm not convinced time always heals, but it calms emotions. Once the anger subsides, the rational mind can get into the game and balance off the emotional mind. It starts as a self-righteous gesture, where the woman graces her cheating man with her presence. The sole purpose is to make sense of his brand of crazy. She needs an understanding of things like what led him to cheat, what made him think he wouldn't get caught, and what made him believe his *playmate* would never tell. Therefore, she is giving him a chance to explain.

She has yet to relinquish her anger, but over time if she keeps dipping in his pool of explanations, she will find herself

## The Truth About The Lies

falling prey to becoming "The Savior." Right now, the only hope he has is to oblige, so he gladly puts up with her attitude. Her righteous indignation leaves her hesitant to listen to what she considers useless excuses from a liar of a man. However, she is eager to hear how he will justify his actions and plead his case. Her initial approach is more like a prosecuting attorney in a sensational criminal case. Using his words, thoughts, and confessions to shame him into feeling like a low-down dirty dog gives her gratification.

The first conversation leaves him feeling like a deer caught in headlights. The wound that his cheating created turned into anger, and the anger has now converted to self-righteousness. She blows a fuse, and the conversation turns into one that allows her to say what she needs to say instead of listening to what he wants to say. Once she totally unloads, she exits without giving him the luxury of a response. Conversation number two plays out a bit differently. Still, in the manner of a prosecuting attorney, she meticulously selects the battery of questions. Her intent is to shred to pieces his every explanation, excuse, and justification for cheating.

While "The Savior" has been shifting gears between being self-righteous and the prosecutor, her man has been on a mission of his own. His primary goal in allowing her to flog him has always been to convince her not to end the relationship. He thinks that if he's successful, she will put her guard down and give him another chance. He has continued to profess his love for her, his remorse for cheating, and his insight into what has to change if given a chance. He assures her he has learned his lesson and is persistent in telling her how empty his life will be without her. His goal is to continue until he has worn her down and she gives him a chance to change.

Let's look at how "The Savior" forms. Two choirs are singing different tunes in her ear. One sings to the tune of *"he ain't worth it; you deserve better; and you can never trust a cheater"* while the other chants, *"he's learned his lesson; he looks so sad, and he must really love you to allow you to put him through all of this."* These conflicting thoughts give way to the birth of "The Savior." When she thinks this is what they needed all along to help build a stronger commitment, it's a done deal. Against her better judgment and reservations, she gives in to his begging, plotting, and manipulation. She compiles a list of "do's and don'ts" to present to him as her

## I Have To Give Him A Chance To Change

bible with the commandments on how to keep her. She is morphing into "The Savior."

The trouble with this *change thing* is she expects her man to change according to her instructions and demands. She never intends to give him the chance to show her how he has changed. All he needs to do is read her bible and follow her commandments. This is where she becomes "The Savior" because now that she has given him another chance, she makes herself responsible for his change. She becomes his moral compass, his decision-maker, his teacher, and his event planner. She is not ready to take a chance on him changing on his own. Her commandments have been issues, and he needs to follow the script.

Of course, this experiment will fail. "The Savior" has laid out her version of *The Relationship Commandments*, and she expects her cheating man to show her he has changed by following them to the letter. This is the only change she wants to see; anything short of total compliance is unacceptable. With this plan, either he does what she has laid out, or he can get out of her life. She will leave nothing to chance.

If she wanted to give him a chance, she would take cues from his actions to assess his true readiness to change. She would observe what he is self-motivated to do differently without manipulation. The only way she will know if he has changed would be to allow him the time, opportunity, and platform to show change or lack thereof. Instead, she has made the mold and now intends to pour in the man. That's the only way she feels she can know the change she gets is the change she wants.

The Truth is, she doesn't care that he is incapable of changing on his own as long as he obeys her commandments. She trusts her commandments will guarantee them a successful relationship, and since she is *giving him a chance to change,* it is his duty to carry out every one of them. I've said it before, genuine change comes from within. If she has to manufacture change in him, she is just setting herself up to be cheated on again. He will be a cheater attempting to honor a list of commandments and not a changed man.

She is lying to herself and to her cheating man about giving him a chance to change. The Truth is, she is giving him a chance to *perform*. Her need to lay down the law and become the deputy of his actions shows a lack of trust. Remember, when "The Savior" made her list of the most important things needed for a healthy relationship; *trust* was at the top of the list. She said *trust* was the cornerstone of a successful relationship, and a relationship without trust is impossible. Well then, it goes without saying, her list of commandments will not rebuild the trust needed for her to reconnect with her man. Therefore, she is lying when she says she is giving him a chance to change. The Truth is, at best, their relationship will become mechanical because it will require constant manipulation to work.

From her core, she knows that she cannot trust him to change. She is simply trying to create some sense of security within herself by giving him the commandments and being his moral compass. Because of his true character, she knows that he will not change on his own accord or by his own free will. She knew what would happen if she didn't provide him with a list of commandments because he has cheated before. Left on his own, he cheated again, so this time she's not willing to gamble on him changing. So, when she says, *I have to give him a chance to change;* she means that literally. The Truth is, she is not giving him a chance to change. She is giving him a chance to show that he can follow a list of instructions, and that keeps her stuck with her cheating man.

# PART 8

# LIES

# "THE COMPROMISER"

## TELLS HERSELF

# HE TAKES CARE OF ME

After finding out about a man's cheating, and emotions have run the course, the woman develops the *art* of compromising. Compromising, to cope, is simply a bargaining tool used to make something you experience as unsettling seem reasonable. It is the brain bargaining with the emotions, while the head is bargaining with the heart. It is a concession of principles. *Bargaining* grows into the give and take, the pros and cons, and the costs versus the benefits. Why would a woman logically stay? What could she possibly gain from staying with a repeat cheater? Will staying cost or benefit her more? "The Compromiser" will create uncomfortable-comfort, negative-positivity, and lose-win circumstances with a cheating man.

Compromising starts with the foundational belief, *"He Takes Care of Me."* Who doesn't want to be taken care of in a relationship? The woman arranges an arsenal of lies around the belief that she is staying because her cheating man takes care of her. Her misconception allows her to create a win for herself after she has suffered a major loss from his cheating. The list of things she focuses on to create her win, in a losing situation, looks something like this:

- He has a good job.
- He takes me to nice places.
- He pays the bills.
- He gives me money for nice *things*.
- He fixes and/or takes care of *thing*s.
- He provides for the *things* I need.
- He makes sure *things* are in order.

If "The Compromiser" would write this stuff down and inspect what she is giving him credit for doing, she would see that he takes care of things and not her. Being *provided for* and being *taken care of* are two totally different things. To make a case for staying with him, she has attempted to make them the same. There is an enormous difference, and if she took the time to differentiate between the two, she could not build a case for staying. That is why she employs the *art of compromising* rather than the *science of observation.* Art is abstract and creative, while science is fact-based and literal.

Let's break it down—being *provided for* means, she has tangible evidence of her man's presence in her life. He wants her to have nice things and to have what she needs. She "represents" for him to "the people" that he is a good man, so he provides her with things that will show his worth. Her man might be a cheater, but he holds an image of himself as responsible and honorable. He believes in old school values of a man providing for his woman, and he does that well. Providing for her is more about his image of himself than his connection to her.

Does "The Compromiser" even know what *being taken care of* looks or feels like? To take care of something, you need the knowledge of what it needs to thrive and what it takes to be its best. To take care of something you need to know the "do's and don'ts" that go along with its care. You also have to pay attention to how it responds to what you do, be in-tune and be willing to make adjustments as needed. Taking care of something means you take the time to get to know how it operates. Learn the signs that indicate when what you are doing is not working and when you are doing something right. If this is not how she is being treated, then he is not taking care of her.

"The Compromiser" is aware that her man cheats, and she has stayed anyway. Does his cheating hurt? Sure it does. The list of things he does "to take care of her" is medicine for her wounds. If she can keep a long list, she can continue to justify her decision to stay. She will not have to face the reality that her man is not in-tune with her, nor connected to her and therefore, not caring for her if she can continue to focus on all the things he does for her. If she can keep her focus on the list of things he provides for her, she won't have to deal with the spiritual disconnect she feels when lying to herself and going against her value system.

The Truth is, focusing on what her man does *for her* and not *to her* keeps "The Compromiser" from admitting what matters to her does not matter to him. It matters very much to her that he cheats, but he continues to be unfaithful. It matters that he does not honor her values, but he continues to violate her boundaries. She continues to nurse the idea of him taking care of her, so she does not have to face the fact that the only one he is taking care of is "himself." If the things he gives and does are enough to make her proud to be his woman, then she should continue to compromise. If she has made peace with his cheating because of what he provides, then "The Compromiser" should continue on her journey with her cheating man.

The Truth is, the danger in hiding behind the lie that he takes care of her gives her man a permit to continue to cheat. It gives him a sense of entitlement to continue to pleasure himself. He will have to give her more and more for her to mask the fact that she is compromising her true wants and desires for things that represent *being taken care of*. The Truth is, continuing to believe the lie puts her at risk of compromising too much for too long. The hope is eventually, she will realize the truth that her man does not take care of her. Once she accepts the fact that he is not taking care of her, she can begin to take care of herself by releasing the lie.

The uncomfortable-comfort, negative-positivity, and lose-win situations she has formulated enable her to stay. His cheating creates uncomfortable emotions that are offset by the comfort of practical thinking. The heart is uncomfortable, but the head has a measure of comfort. She is uncomfortable with the fact she is staying with a cheater, and this creates negative emotions. However, finding comfort in the things he provides creates practical and positive reasons to stay. The negative-positivity of the matter is this is neither the life she wants, nor would have chosen, but she brainwashes herself into finding security in the things he gives and provides for her needs. It's a lose-win situation at its best because she knows he is cheating but, by becoming "The Compromiser," she has developed the ability to offset the damage by accepting the things he gives and provides as restitution for his unfaithfulness.

The Truth is, she will have to master the art of choosing what she wants to see instead of seeing what is happening in order to stay with him. She will have to be minimally alert at all times meaning, she will purposefully overlook the obvious, continuous betrayals to feel he is taking care of her. She cannot acknowledge the emotional pain felt each time she slips back into consciousness because that shatters the illusion of "being taken care of."

The Truth is, he cannot possibly simultaneously violate and take care of her at the same time. He is not taking care of her. In reality, he is providing for her needs while continuing to take care of himself. Until she accepts this, she will stay stuck with her cheating man whom she needs to believe takes care of her.

# EVERYBODY HAS TO DEAL WITH SOMETHING IN THEIR RELATIONSHIP

Have you been in the presence of someone reflecting on their man's cheating who ends up rationalizing the situation by saying something like, *"everybody has to deal with something in their relationship because there are no perfect people?"* Although there are no perfect people, there is a person who is perfect for you. Our needs vary, and what we need in our partner varies accordingly. Everyone is looking for something unique when they enter a relationship, but we all want the same things; to feel appreciated, respected, and valued. Cheating creates the opposite of these feelings in a relationship.

The route to feeling appreciated, respected, and valued is unique to each woman and depends on her experiences. Her individual relationship histories created the scars, heartaches, and regrets that have developed into her current needs. The cheating in previously failed relationships has morphed into the needs she seeks to fulfill in current situations. These needs govern what she will tolerate in her new relationship. At least that's how boundaries develop until "The Compromiser" is birthed.

It often takes some time for her to get to the place where she acknowledges that things will not work as she had hoped. When she is busy trying to get her needs met, she enters a zone that blinds her and distorts her perception of the truth. She sees it and doesn't see it. She knows something is not right, but plows straight past all the big orange cones straight into the hazardous zone. "The Compromiser" is being formed, and she doesn't even know it.

How does she miss the signs while she is turning into "The Compromiser?" It's simple; it takes time to build a solid foundation for a healthy, satisfying, monogamous relationship. While in the foundation-building phase of the relationship, still gathering information about her man, she doesn't consider it a compromise when choosing to *"see something and not see it."* She considers the relationship a work-in-progress, and she is analyzing the information gathered about her man so she can later determine what matters. Next, a give-and-take mentality emerges to propel her forward because she doesn't want to be demanding, nagging, or controlling. This is the beginning of the compromising that she will end up continuing to stay in this relationship.

As time passes, her ability to see exactly *"what is"* sharpens. The give-and-take mentality now gives way to the ability to acknowledge flaws in the relationship. Because "The Compromiser" believes there is hope for improvement, she stays in the relationship believing she can fix him. Now she weighs the costs of leaving to the benefits of staying and comparing his flaws against his strengths. What woman in a compromising position has not taken out a piece of paper, drawn a line down the middle, and labeled one side *pros* and the other *cons*? This is the beginning of the phase where she bargains with herself about whether to stay in the relationship with a cheater or to leave. "The Compromiser" is born at this phase in the relationship.

If she is honest with herself, she will have to admit the cons have outweighed the pros. The Truth is, this awareness made taking an inventory necessary. She knows that things are not right, and she has been putting up with undesirable situations. She no longer feels honored in the relationship. However, "The Compromiser" is not ready to walk away, but her vision has sharpened to where she can see *"what is."* She has to settle this internal battle and needs to be sure it justifies her to stay. So, she makes a detailed list of pros to validate her decision. She might as well save herself some time and flip a coin because the odds are about the same.

Instead of dealing head-on with the fact that she is with a cheater, she adapts to generalizing. She nurses the belief that *"everybody has to deal with something in their relationship,"* and this is the *"something"* that she will have to deal with. Now here is how the compromiser mentality builds muscle. She goes back down relationship memory lane and pulls out all the vile, deceptive, and disrespectful things that her past partners did. Next, she compares what they did to what her current man hasn't done. The comparison game continues with a review of what her girlfriends have put up with compared to what she is dealing with, and what her coworkers complain about compared to her gripes about her man. She determines that her situation is not nearly as bad as theirs, and therefore, she will stay with her cheating man because *"everybody has to deal with something in their relationship."*

If other's real-life drama isn't enough to convince her that her situation is not that bad, she turns to celebrity gossip and public drama to support her belief. After combing through tabloids, social media, and talk shows, she has gathered enough evidence to support her belief that *"everybody has to deal with something in their relationship."* The Truth is, she does not base her decision to stay on her true feelings. She has worked very hard to build a case to support her self-betrayal. She betrayed her values, forfeited self-respected, and accepted the unacceptable because of the faulty comparison game she has been playing. "The Compromiser" is in full bloom. She decides that her *compromise* will be to settle for his cheating because the comparison game has convinced her that things could be so much worse.

What happens when "dealing with something" starts to deal with her? What happens when "dealing with something" starts to diminish her level of well-being, self-worth, and self-confidence? What happens when she continuously has to re-write the script to fit the circumstances she finds herself in rather than rely on her true values as her guide? What happens when all possibilities of forcing the relationship to be one that fosters feelings of appreciation, respect, and value have been exhausted? What happens when she reaches for her list of pros and cons and realizes the cons far outweigh the pros? Maybe what will happen is, she will finally be ready to stop lying to herself and face the truth about the relationship with her cheating man.

When he cheated the first time, she used the pros and cons list to assist with her decision of whether to stay or leave. She stayed because she gave her man's cheating far less weight on the list than she should have. Cheating was more than likely a huge deal-breaker in her past relationships and a reason to leave. As fate would have it, cheating had been an issue in relationship after relationship until she compromised on the weight of the offense. Undoubtedly, there are some women who can deal with men cheating without it diminishing their sense of well-being, worth, and confidence. They believe that all men cheat and therefore cheating for them is not a deal-breaker. Then, there are the women who experience cheating in such an intense way that to "deal with it" starts to "deal with them." "The Compromiser" has to be honest about which category she falls within.

If staying with her cheating man means she will have to minimize the significance and impact of his cheating on her well-being, then she will have to lie to herself to stay. The Truth is, her choices are, to be honest with herself about the non-negotiable nature of cheating as it relates to her core values, or to create a self-deceptive means of dealing with it. *Everybody has to deal with something in their relationship,* but what she deals with shouldn't result in her having to lie to herself about the weight of it on her spirit. Deceiving herself about the weight of his cheating becomes a lie that gets harder and harder to deal with each time he cheats. The Truth is, his cheating has killed something inside her soul and destroyed a part of her spirit that can never be resuscitated. No matter how often she lies, "The Compromiser" can't fool herself into believing the needs he is meeting outweigh the impact of his cheating on her spirit.

How does the spirit die from self-deception? There is a bit of shame that develops in an attempt to pass off what you don't want as what you can accept. There is a false sense of confidence that develops from having what she tells herself is an acceptable compromise for her actual needs. A nagging sense of discontentment keeps her longing for genuine needs to be met. It is hard for her to pretend to be comfortable with her man repeatedly violating her boundaries. This is how the spirit dies a slow death while the relationship survives.

Has the primary need to be in a healthy, monogamous, mutually exclusive relationship died, or is her lie keeping her stuck with her cheating man? *"Everybody has to deal with something"* is like a cast that "The Compromiser" wraps around the fractured relationship to hold it together. What is mutually exclusive is the fact that she cannot deal with the truth of the relationship and stay true to her values at the same time. If she hasn't been able to heal from her man's cheating, and the wounds are still tender, then the cheating is dealing with her instead of her dealing with it. She is lying to herself about being able to accept it as *something* that she can deal with in her relationship.

Compromising her true value system to incorporate a false acceptance of cheating is a hard change to achieve. It is a cover-up and a fraud to her true self. It is a compromise of who she is. It is her wanting to accept her man's cheating as a trade-off for accepting the fact that everybody has to deal with something in their relationship. It is a lie, and there are few things more damaging to her spirit than self-deception.

Self-deception demands that she manipulate events and circumstances to fit into the scope of the lie. It attempts to fool her into believing her needs are being met and what she isn't getting isn't as important. It makes the reality a lie and the lie a reality. It creates a need in her that is greater than the need for the truth, and this feeds the self-deception and keeps her stuck. The Truth is, the self-deception that leads to her lies is more damaging than the betrayal experienced by his cheating.

What really hurts "The Compromiser" is not solely her man's cheating. Attempting to accept the lie that his cheating is *"the something"* she has to deal with actually starts to deal with her. Each time he deceives and betrays her, she has to turn up her self-deception to magnify the lie that this is something she can deal with. This is just like trying to pass off something counterfeit as something real. Think about a person who buys counterfeit products. They either can't pay, don't believe they can pay, or don't want to pay the price for the real thing. They obviously want the real thing or else they would not be flaunting the counterfeit version. However, they settle for a fake version of the genuine thing. Surely, they know it is not real, but they carry it as if it were. This is a perfect example of what "The Compromiser" is doing when she lies about being able to accept her man's cheating.

The Truth is, choosing to deal with the unacceptable eventually backfires. Slowly but consistently, it will make her forget she deserves an honest man. She will forget that she deserves to be in an exclusive, monogamous relationship. "The Compromiser" will believe there are no men who value fidelity. The lie causes her to forget how healthy, intimate relationships should feel. All of this is the *"something"* that she will be stuck dealing with. She will forget, although there are no perfect relationships, there is a relationship that is perfect for her. "The Compromiser" should meditate on the truth until it leads her to deal with her man's cheating in a way that is not "dealing" with her.

# AS LONG AS HE'S RESPECTFUL WITH HIS CHEATING I DON'T CARE

When I was a young girl, I fondly remember sitting on my grandmother's porch as the evening fell. The elder women from the neighborhood would gather there to "spill the tea." There was nothing like good ol' gossip about who was caught with whom, who was suspected of creeping with whom, and who was trying to hook-up whom. It was as if they took pride in knowing all the neighborhood gossip. They may have had differing opinions about the tea that was spilled, but they all agreed on one thing; as long as their men were respectful with their cheating, they couldn't care less.

The elder compromisers would say things like, *"as long as he doesn't flaunt his women in my face," "as long as he keeps his dirt in the streets," and "as long as he takes care of home, I don't care if he cheats."* I could never understand how a woman could say she didn't care about her man cheating, no matter what the circumstances. They all believed there was such a thing as "respectful cheating." To this day, I have never understood how being "respectful" and "cheating" could exist at the same time.

Even as a young girl enjoying "grown folks' talk," I knew that cheating was disrespectful. Is it possible to keep the cheating "respectful," "in the streets," and "out of your house?" The elder compromiser might have turned a blind eye to her man's cheating because nobody had to know as long as he was careful to cover his tracks. This is not the case with the current day compromisers because social media has blown the lid off many affairs. The current-day compromiser has to deal with what her man is doing in the streets through vicious Facebook and Instagram posts that are never respectful. Her man might take the liberty to text or FaceTime the other woman while she is in another room. All too often she discovers that the cheater had texted his mistress while sitting right next to or lying in the bed with her. These behaviors are disrespectful and make their way off the streets right into her home. Where is the respect?

# The Truth About The Lies

If you cheated in school, you would get into trouble. If you cheated while playing a game, it would disqualify you. If you cheated someone out of money, you would have to repay the debt. Common synonyms for cheating are trick, deceive, dishonest, unfair, defraud, scam, and dupe. Cheating has always been wrong on all accounts and has carried a negative consequence, so how could the elder women reach the point of not caring about their men cheating? It is because they spent their lives *compromising* that they had grown to not care. The elder women nursed the lie about what was acceptable for such a long time that they created a respectful version of cheating.

The current day compromiser remembers the words of her elders and therefore believes the impossible to be possible. Because of what she endured while staying with her cheater, she has revised her rulebook. She fails to acknowledge the fact that it is impossible to be respectful of your partner and cheat at the same time. How can a man take care of his home while cheating at the same time? Cheating is a demonstration of blatant dishonesty. It is an act of disregarding and dishonoring a commitment to your partner. There is no respect in that.

This lie has been passed down from generation to generation, and the elder compromisers have tainted the innocent minds of the younger women. Maybe the belief, "as long as he's respectful with his cheating I don't care" kept the divorce rate down back in the day. Possibly this belief kept women from experiencing depression, anxiety, and emotional instability. Their choice to compromise in this way no doubt created the nonsense that we so often hear quoted, "a man will be a man."

The Truth is, "The Compromiser" has rewarded her man for being slick with his cheating. She has given him a pass for creeping lightly and has mislabeled it "respectful." The problem is when she can no longer maintain the lie that she doesn't care about his cheating as long as he is respectful, she will start unraveling. The inability to accept cheating has led *compromisers* into the office of a counselor, preacher, or psychiatrist. The realization of the inability to *"respectfully cheat"* has contributed to women experiencing emotional and mental disturbance. "The Compromiser" ends up seeking help to deal with the cheating once she realizes there is no such thing as "respectful cheating."

Let's examine how "The Compromiser" arrived at the

place where she could consider there being a respectful way to cheat. The first time her man cheated, she felt disrespected, betrayed, and used. She was confused about how he pulled it off, how she missed the signs, and how naïve she was for trusting him. Respectful cheating was the furthest thing from her thinking. However, when she stayed with her cheater, she had to make sense of it, and make it feel sane. What she did was create a new set of boundaries and some new expectations so she could rewrite her rules. "The Compromiser" wrote the book and gave him the manuscript on how to cheat respectfully.

That's right, "The Compromiser" actually taught her man how to "respectfully cheat." She had no control over whether he would cheat again, and she knew this. The only way she could control whether he cheated again would be to end their relationship. She stayed and created some restrictions on cheating that described what she could stomach. The Truth is, she taught her man how to "respectfully cheat" so she could respect herself for staying.

The continuous cheating leads to continuous bargaining and renegotiating boundaries. The negotiating goes a bit like this, *"well he respects me enough to never _____, and he hasn't done _____ out of respect for me, plus he's careful to never allow her to _____, which I could never live with, so as long as he's respectful with his cheating, I don't care."* By the time "The Compromiser" finishes navigating through her maze of self-deception, she accepts the lie that there is a respectful way to cheat. She eliminates some of her original boundaries that deemed cheating as totally unacceptable. The word "respectful" has to be redefined to allow her to stay with her cheating man.

It is said that history repeats itself. The current-day compromiser may be creative enough to delude herself into believing the lie about the existence of "respectful cheating." If she can, she may avoid experiencing emotional and mental disturbance. The result will be her taking on the mentality of the elder compromisers. She will carry on the age-old tradition of staying with her man and not caring if he cheats as long as he is respectful. The misfortunes of other women will strengthen her false sense of confidence and acceptance. Each time she witnesses or hears about a man *"disrespectfully cheating"* she validates her choice to stay with her man who cares enough about her to respectfully cheat.

## The Truth About The Lies

A false sense of confidence and acceptance is what she gets for her belief. A false sense of respect is what she gets from exploiting other women's misery for her validation. She develops a false sense of setting boundaries from deceiving herself into believing that the limits she sets for his cheating equate to anything respectful. The lie conjures up a false sense of pride from pitying the women who are not as lucky as she is to have a respectful cheater. The Truth is, what she has created is a false sense of reality.

Now, let's process the lie, *"I don't care."* She professes to not care that her man is cheating as long as he is respectful. Really, who doesn't care that their man is cheating? Isn't it every woman's dream to have the ideal, committed relationship with her man? Is cheating a component of any woman's ideal vision of commitment? Could "The Compromiser" be lying to herself about not caring because her man cheats "respectfully?" Does a distorted perception of respect contribute to her lack of care? What would be different if she cared?

Honestly, what self-respecting woman would not care that her man is cheating? *I don't care* minimizes her ability to attend to her own needs, wants, and sense of self-worth. What self-respecting woman can take pride in vowing to stay with her cheating man? "The Compromiser" can never honor the fact that she accepts his cheating "as long as he's respectful." She has bargained and compromised her way into being stuck with him. The Truth is, she can honestly say her man cheats following the rules she has set, and maybe she respects that.

The Truth about the situation is she has set the stage for him to not honor or respect her. Her attempt to manipulate his actions into a pattern of cheating that she can accept sets her up to be blind to her genuine need for fidelity, loyalty, and respect. She has disregarded herself to make his cheating respectful. I wonder what would happen if she honored her values instead of her man's ability to cheat respectfully? The Truth is, if she stays with him, she can never honor her values. She will end up stuck with a cheating man just like the *elder compromisers* from her childhood memories. History is repeating itself, and she will pass the delusion of respectful cheating down to create the next generation of compromisers.

# EPILOGUE

What would it be like to live in truth? The purpose of challenging the lies that keep women stuck with cheating men has been to enhance the ability to accept your role in the current circumstances. Each section was written to spark self-evaluation to render you less susceptible to self-deception. The ultimate goal is for you to develop the capacity to live in truth. When you tear down the walls of self-deception, you are much better prepared to create the relationship you want with yourself and your man. Choosing the most appropriate man to share your life with will become second nature when you tell the truth about the lies.

Experiencing the empowerment that comes from living in truth should be every woman's desire. Living in truth leads to feeling confident, while living a lie leads to feeling insecure. Living in truth leads to feeling complete, while living a lie leads to feeling fragmented. Reflecting on the past, by tearing down the walls that support the lies that have kept you stuck, is the beginning of living in your truth. Imagine being able to confidently and boldly accept only what you want, need, and value in your life. Joy and peace will be what you experience when ceasing to violate your boundaries and compromise your self-worth.

Living in truth is to acknowledge life *"as is,"* without distorting your reality. It is to deal only with *"what is."* When you live in truth, you can see *"what is"* and honestly ask yourself if this is what you want. The lies you tell lead your life down a deceptive path where you have to fight hard to turn what isn't, and never will be, into what you want. It is not only the relationship *"as is"* or the partner *"as is"* that creates your pain, discomfort, and stagnation. It is also the lies you tell and your distorted view of reality that significantly contributes to your suffering. You share the responsibility because of the lies you have embraced to manipulate a partner and relationship into what you want but cannot have because of *"what is."*

## The Truth About The Lies

There is no loss in living in truth, but there is major loss in living a lie. Just take a minute to think about what you experience when lies exist. Lies create fear and result in the preoccupation with covering up the truth. They create a lack of security and comfort which keeps you on edge. Lies take on a life of their own and lead you further away from the truth. Relationships become messy when you lie to yourself about *"what is."*

When you embrace the truth, it is not personal; creating lies personalizes things. The truth is uncompromising, clear, and only reflects *"what is"* in its purest form. When dealing with the truth, you do not have to fix or distort what is, you simply have to accept or choose not to accept it. The lie is what magnifies feelings of being betrayed, used, and deceived. Lies intensify the feeling of not being good enough and lead to stagnation. The Truth leads to progression and corrects twisted beliefs and perceptions. Develop the courage to tell the truth and start to live for you. Your journey to becoming unstuck begins here.